IN THE KITCHEN
WITH
AINSLEY HARRIOTT
OVER 100 DELICIOUSLY
SIMPLE RECIPES

With photographs by
Philip Webb

BBC Books

NOTES ON RECIPES

ALL THE RECIPES IN THIS BOOK HAVE BEEN TESTED.
FOLLOW ONE SET OF MEASUREMENTS ONLY. DO NOT MIX METRIC AND IMPERIAL.
USE SIZE 3 EGGS EXCEPT WHERE A LARGE EGG IS NEEDED, THEN USE SIZE 1 OR 2.
SPOON MEASURES ARE LEVEL UNLESS OTHERWISE STATED.
USE UNWAXED LEMONS IF POSSIBLE WHEN RECIPES INCLUDE LEMON RIND.
RECIPES SUITABLE FOR VEGETARIANS (NOT INCLUDING DESSERTS) ARE MARKED WITH A (V)
SYMBOL. PLEASE NOTE THAT THESE MAY CONTAIN CHEESE OR OTHER DAIRY PRODUCTS.

Published by BBC Books,
an imprint of BBC Worldwide Publishing,
BBC Worldwide Limited,
Woodlands, 80 Wood Lane,
London W12 0TT

First published in 1996

Photographs by Philip Webb
Home economist: Sarah Ramsbottom
Stylist: Clare-Louise Hunt
Design: DW Design

© Ainsley Harriott, 1996

The moral rights of the author have been asserted

ISBN 0 563 38720 3

Typeset by Phoenix Photosetting, Chatham, Kent
Colour Reproduction by Radstock Reproductions Ltd, Midsomer Norton
Printed by Martins the Printers Ltd, Berwick-upon-Tweed
Bound by Hunter & Foulis Ltd, Edinburgh
Colour printing by Lawrence Allen Ltd, Weston-super-Mare
Cover printed by Clays Ltd, St Ives plc

CONTENTS

From the first moment my mother handed me a spoon covered in cake mix, my tastebuds yearned for new flavours. Perhaps this was the reason for me taking such an early interest in food. I would gladly mix, beat, whip and occasionally scissor my way around the kitchen, just to be where the action was. In our house, mum was constantly in the kitchen as people were always popping in or visiting from abroad. For me, the kitchen became an extension of the playroom and it wasn't long before I was cooking cakes for schoolfriends, often, as my mother used to say, eating her out of house and home.

opportunity to talk proudly about how I had prepared and created the meal and their enjoyment gave me a lot of satisfaction and confidence – the key word here being confidence. Don't feel inhibited: cooking has so much to offer and the fun element is tasting new things and learning how to trust your palate.

Also, make the kitchen a fun place to be. Decorate it with colours that make *you* feel good, not necessarily those you see in trendy magazines. Give yourself space to work in so you can be more efficient and this will give you more time to relax

INTRODUCTION

My early experiences of cooking, apart from giving me immense pleasure, also taught me discipline in the kitchen. I learned that even mundane things like shopping could be fun as I could identify things I had cooked with. Washing up was easy, as I got to lick the bowl, and most important of all, I was more inclined to eat green vegetables because I had helped to prepare them. If you've got children, and the time to educate them, then cooking is one of the most wonderful social skills to have.

Going into the catering industry opened my eyes to a whole new world of food and temperamental chefs. I quickly learnt how important it was to have standards and not to be afraid to express yourself. Cooking for family and friends at home gave me the

with your family and friends.

It is also a good idea to invest in the right kitchen equipment. We spend a great deal of time in the kitchen preparing and cooking food and a few good kitchen tools will make cooking more enjoyable and a lot easier, too.

INGREDIENTS

In The Kitchen With Ainsley Harriott offers you lots of variety and, I hope, lots of enjoyment. We're very lucky, here in Britain, to be able to buy a wide variety of produce from around the world which is generally available all year round in almost perfect condition and I have reflected this in the recipes in this book.

Fresh tropical fruits never seem to be off the shelves. Even fresh strawberries can be bought on a freezing day in January, though the imported American and Dutch varieties sometimes taste like eating a piece of velvet and, I have to say, you can't beat an English strawberry.

There's a whole new range of fish available now and, although I've only concentrated on a few species here, you can always alter the recipe by using a different fish. Don't forget that fishmongers will do any cleaning or boning for you, you simply have to ask. Always check that the fish you buy is fresh: the skin should glisten and be slightly slimy, the eyes clear and transparent, the gills bright and red and, most important of all, it should not smell fishy. If it does, it's going off, or it's at least well on the way.

Meat is another product that can be cut and prepared practically any way you want. Your butcher will trim off any excess fat – you may have to pay extra for the pre-cut meat, but it's well worth it if you want a healthier cut. When selecting beef, look for meat which is darkish red with yellow-tinted fat. Check it away from the bright lights of the supermarket's refrigerated cabinets. Lamb should be deep pink, not grey, and pork should be pink with white fat. Try to buy rindless bacon if possible. Chicken is still the most popular meat and for real flavour you can't beat free range. The meat on the legs is a much deeper pink than the breast and it should smell clean and fresh, not sour. The skin

should be firm and smooth, not sticky. The same applies to turkey.

All of this is very important, especially with regard to the colour of meat that is wrapped in see-through plastic. With all cuts of meat and poultry, don't buy more than you need, only to store it in your fridge for days on end. It's far better to buy a smaller quantity for a few days at a time.

Vegetables right now are very exciting and good value for money. Most supermarkets now offer a previously undreamed-of selection. Remember that vegetables in season are at their best and most natural. Frozen vegetables are okay for an instant meal, but lack the flavour of fresh vegetables, and I rarely buy ready-cut vegetables as they tend to be more expensive than loose ones. If you're not sure how to prepare and cook a certain type of vegetable, ask at the customer service desk in the supermarket or find a good greengrocer. If they've got them in, give them a go; remember what people thought of garlic a few years ago? Foreign muck!! Gone are the days when you could just buy a soft round English lettuce and maybe a Cos in the summer months. Nowadays, the range of lettuce is daunting. Buy two or three contrasting varieties – the different types of lettuce leaves can brighten up any table with wonderful colours, shapes, textures and tastes. You can often buy small pre-washed quantities, but if you do buy whole lettuces, make sure the leaves are tightly packed to save on washing time and damage. Once washed, spin dry and store in sealed plastic bags in the fridge and they'll keep fresh for days.

Tinned tomatoes are great when it comes to price and convenience but, again, there are a huge variety of tomatoes available to most of us at our local supermarket all year round. The stalks, if they are still intact, are a great way of telling how fresh they are: pick them up carefully and smell the stalk – they should smell slightly earthy. Colour is not always a good indication of flavour, but most supermarkets now sell tomatoes 'grown for flavour'. They may be a little more expensive but, after all, flavour is what we're after.

I tend to use olive oil quite a lot. This does not mean you have to follow suit, but olive oil, besides being good for you, actually tastes far superior to your normal, everyday cooking oil. You don't necessarily have to buy the most expensive olive oil, but find one with a good flavour. If you go to a good delicatessen, they should let you taste before you buy. If you buy one from a supermarket, get a small quantity to start with. Extra virgin olive oil is the best as it's obtained from the first pressing of the olives. If you hold it up to the light, it should have a strong green tint to it and it will give your cooking and salad dressings plenty of flavour. Yes, it is very expensive compared to other oils, but you are what you eat, and you're worth it!

Fresh herbs are also important to me. One of the great pleasures of cooking is the wonderful aroma that herbs give off. Certain types go well with particular foods: fresh basil is delightful with tomatoes and pasta, rosemary and sage bring out the flavour of lamb, and fennel and dill flavour fish beautifully. Oregano and marjoram excite pizzas, coriander adds a taste of the Orient to anything and parsley warms to vegetables. The list is endless and if you have the opportunity to grow your own, you'll discover how valuable fresh herbs can be. Although I have not included more unusual herbs like lovage, hyssop or borage, you can always experiment with them, but first you have to get hold of them. Freeze-dried herbs retain their colour better than the normal dried varieties and I'm particularly fond of using freeze-dried oregano.

I've occasionally used dried herbs and if that's all you have available when the recipe calls for fresh, reduce the quantity by half. There are herbs that don't dry particularly well, especially basil, chervil, chives and parsley. They taste and look nothing like the real thing, so try and search out the fresh. It's always better to buy them fresh and then wash them, chop them up, pop them in small, well-sealed plastic bags and store them in your freezer, but don't forget, stored herbs lose their aromatic qualities after a time. Cooking with cream and butter features quite a lot in the book, even though my wife often says, 'You may as well just slap it on my thighs', but again they are there for maximum flavour. To save some money though, you can always buy cooking butter when you are baking, but when I say double cream, I mean double cream, especially in sauces. If you substitute single cream, the sauce is likely to split or curdle. However crème fraîche or fromage frais, although slightly sharper, work well in sauces and often have a lower fat content.

Always make sure that your dairy produce is well covered and stored away from strong smelling foods as it can quickly pick up flavours. Cheese is usually eaten with fruit and bread in my house and I like to take it out of the fridge at least an hour before eating to allow the flavours to develop fully. Try to avoid buying ready-grated Parmesan. It's best to buy it in a block and grate it when you need it. This way you get the wonderful pungent aroma rather than cheese resembling and tasting like wood chippings. Always wrap cheese up in greaseproof paper before storing in the fridge as this will reduce the cheesy smell. Although more expensive, I always use free-range eggs.

Most of us rarely have time to make stocks and, as you will see, I've used stock cubes in the recipes. Again, for maximum flavour buy the quality varieties. Look out for supermarket stocks which, although more expensive than a stock cube, will give you more flavour. If you've seen me on *Good Morning*, you'll know that my most trusted friend is Percy the peppermill. I always use freshly ground black pepper and often bring out Suzy saltmill for some freshly ground rock salt. The quantities of seasonings I've used are really only a guide. As your confidence grows, you'll be able to adjust them to suit your taste.

As you will see, I've used tinned pulses instead of fresh, mainly to save on time, but don't be afraid to soak and cook dried pulses as they work out a lot cheaper than tinned.

Pasta comes in all shapes and sizes and, although fresh pasta is widely available, dried pasta is just as good and cheaper. Have some fun experimenting with the different varieties.

I've tried to keep all the recipes as straightforward as possible, simplicity being paramount. If you feel like adding something or changing it to your own tastes, do so. I've included plenty of alternatives at the start of the recipes. I'm glad to say that I've also included lots of recipes for one person, which are quick, easy and, I hope, thoroughly enjoyable.

EQUIPMENT

With all this information you're almost ready to tackle the recipes, but first let's have a look at what we need in the kitchen.

As I mentioned earlier, your kitchen should be a relaxed, comfortable place. Surround yourself with things that make you feel good to make cooking easier and more pleasurable. Good quality equipment lasts for ages, you'll enjoy using it and, ultimately, it will save you time.

Make sure you have a good work surface area and plenty of space for gadgets you often use i.e. the kettle, toaster and food processor. All the rest can be stored away. Chopping boards are important, so make sure your board is large enough. There's nothing worse than having stuff fall off the edge as you are cutting or your knife not being able to move freely. Put a damp cloth underneath the board to stop it from sliding around and always scrub your boards after use to keep them clean and odour-free, especially wooden ones.

Knives are probably the most important tools in the kitchen. Invest in a good sharp knife – this will not only save you time, it will make cooking more pleasurable. The reason is simple; you need less pressure so the job is smoother and will improve your skills. So please, do yourself a favour and get a good knife, about 20 cm (8 in) long. It should cost between £12–£15 and will last you a lifetime. Why not put it on your Christmas present list? Ideally you should have three different sized knives, the second being a vegetable or paring knife 12 cm (5 in) long and the third a bread knife. Store them in a drawer, away from the children, and never ever leave them in a bowl of water, especially if you're not washing up, just a quick wipe will normally do.

Cooking pots and pans vary enormously from home to home. What you need is a good assortment and remember, the right tool for the right job. Ideally, the perfect selection would be a very large pan for boiling pasta, a couple of large pans with lids for boiling vegetables and rice, a non-stick pan for milk, cream, sauces and custard, a large frying pan or wok with a lid and a small non-stick omelette and pancake pan. For cooking in the oven the selection would include two round or oval ovenproof casserole dishes, a gratin dish and a pie dish for baking, a baking tray, a baking dish, a Swiss roll tin, 20 cm (8 in) flan ring and two sandwich tins, all non-stick to keep life simple. Again, try to buy good quality and they will last you for years and always replace pans with loose handles and worn out bases.

Wooden spoons are very cheap, but even if you build up a collection of different sizes you'll always have your favourite. If you don't have an electric whisk, buy a balloon whisk and a colander (not an old rusty one, often spotted at car boot sales). A rolling pin is essential, especially if you're going to make a lot of pastry, but I've been known on occasions to use a long wine bottle taken out of the fridge instead.

A good vegetable peeler, especially with a swivel blade, is not only easier for both left and right-handed people, it's quicker, and a good sharp pair of kitchen scissors will save time when you're chopping fresh herbs. Measuring jugs and spoons you'll always need and kitchen scales are vitally important when making cakes and desserts. Remember, never, ever mix metric and imperial measurements together.

A food processor makes life so much easier and cuts preparation time to a minimum. Make sure the size you have chosen is right for your needs and follow a few basic rules for good results:

- always add wet ingredients before dry when making things like batters

- mix flour into cake mixtures using the pulse, which gives a quick burst of power
- never overload your food processor, it's more efficient when only half full
- remember your food processor does everything incredibly fast, so keep an eye on it.

Ovens are often the most temperamental things in the kitchen and take a while to get used to. Sometimes dishes come out overdone, other times they are underdone, so next time slightly raise or lower the heat accordingly. Don't be put off cooking, it's often the oven's fault! If you've got a microwave oven, you'll know how useful they are for reheating fast, defrosting, melting butter and chocolate and my children would never forgive me if I didn't mention popcorn. But to avoid any disasters, always read the instruction leaflet and remember the catchphrase: 'Cover it, stir it, rest it, test it' and you won't go far wrong.

Finally, read the recipe carefully before you start so you totally understand it. Pay attention to the level of heat applied for cooking. For example 'simmer gently' means just that, otherwise you'll end up with a burnt pan. Take similar care when grilling. If you decide to flambé something, don't panic when the flames flicker – you're only burning off the alcohol and it will soon die down. Remember that garnishing food can make your dish look exquisite, feeding the eyes and getting the juices flowing. Happy cooking!

SALADS

AINSLEY'S WARM **WINTER** SALAD

SERVES 4

50 g (2 oz) butter
4 tablespoons olive oil
2 cloves garlic, peeled and finely chopped
2 slices bread, white or granary, cut into 1 cm (½ in) cubes
400 g (14 oz) tin artichoke hearts, drained and halved
6 rashers streaky bacon or back bacon
200 g (7 oz) packet mixed lettuce leaves
1 tablespoon snipped fresh chives
FETA CHEESE DRESSING:
6 tablespoons lemon juice
8 tablespoons olive oil
3 tablespoons crème fraîche
50 g (2 oz) feta cheese, crumbled
freshly ground black pepper

There's nothing like a salad whether it's the summer or winter, although being able to get attractive lettuce all year round certainly helps in the winter. Streaky bacon is easiest to crisp, but you can use back bacon if necessary.

The origin of the word salad is the Latin *sal* or 'salt'. It came from the ancient Roman habit of dipping greens in salt before eating. My dad still does it to this day.

METHOD

First make the dressing. Whisk together the lemon juice and oil then, gradually, add the crème fraîche, feta cheese and black pepper. Set aside.

Heat the butter and oil in a frying pan over a low heat. Before the butter starts to brown, add the garlic and cook for about a minute. Add the bread (croûtons), increase the heat and fry until golden brown. Remember to keep the croûtons on the move the whole time using a spatula or wooden spoon, or, if you fancy, short little tosses of the frying pan (but watch for splashes). Remove the croûtons with a slotted spoon when they are golden brown and drain on kitchen paper.

Add the artichoke halves to the same pan and fry on high heat for 2–3 minutes until golden and cripsy on the outside.

Grill the bacon until it is very crisp and crumbled into pieces. Arrange the salad leaves on four serving plates. Scatter the artichoke hearts and croûtons over each plate, then spoon on the dressing. Sprinkle over the crispy bacon and top with the snipped chives and a twist of black pepper.

PINKY GRAPEFRUIT, PRAWNS & GREENY AVOCADO SALAD

SERVES 4

2 pink grapefruits

2 ripe medium-sized avocados

200 g (7 oz) packet mixed lettuce leaves (iceberg/cos/sweet romaine)

100 g (4 oz) cooked peeled prawns

½ red pepper, seeded and cut into fine strips

DRESSING:

6 tablespoons light olive oil

1 tablespoon white wine vinegar

¼ teaspoon ground allspice

1 teaspoon chopped fresh coriander

This combination works so well that it's a big favourite in the Harriott household.

You can use ordinary white grapefruit if you wish – either choice is quite delicious.

Light olive oil is taken from the third or fourth pressing of the olives but still retains more flavour – and is healthier – than ordinary cooking oil.

METHOD

Peel and carefully segment the grapefruit – over a bowl to catch the juice – then squeeze out the juices from the core and skin. Put the juice to one side. Cut the avocados in half, remove the stones and peel off the skin. Then cut each half into 3 slices lengthways. Place the lettuce leaves on 4 serving plates, arrange 3 slices of avocado on top of each serving and divide the grapefruit segments between them. Scatter over the prawns and the strips of red pepper.

To make the dressing, vigorously whisk together the grapefruit juice, oil, vinegar, allspice and coriander until well mixed. Drizzle over the salad before serving. To stay with the pink theme, serve with a glass of kir (cassis and white wine).

ROASTED PEPPER AND PINE NUT SALAD Ⓥ

SERVES 4

450 g (1 lb) pasta shells

3 small mixed peppers (red, green and yellow)

3 tablespoons pine nuts

6 tablespoons virgin olive oil

2 tablespoons garlic vinegar

1 tablespoon chopped chives

salt and freshly ground black pepper

Roasted peppers are really delicious either in salads like this one, or on a slice of toasted garlic bread.

METHOD

Cook the pasta shells in a saucepan until al dente, so the pasta still has some bite to it. Drain and set on one side.

Pre-heat the oven to gas mark 9, 475°F, 240°C. Cut the peppers in half, remove the seeds and brush the outsides with a little oil. Place in a hot oven for about 5–6 minutes until the skin goes dark and starts to blister. Cool, then peel off the skin and cut into 5 mm (¼ in) strips.

Toast the pine nuts under the grill until light golden brown making sure you occasionally shake the tray to get a nice even colour. Whisk the olive oil, vinegar and chives together, then season well.

Mix the pasta shells with the peppers and pine nuts then pour over the dressing. Toss well, add a touch more pepper and serve.

CRUNCHY SMOKED BACON **AND** NEW POTATO **SALAD**

750 g (1½ lb) new potatoes (about the size of a small egg)

225 g (8 oz) smoked bacon, rinded and diced

2 tablespoons sunflower oil

2 tablespoons cider vinegar

1 small red chilli pepper, seeded and finely chopped

salt and freshly ground black pepper

3 spring onions

1 tablespoon chopped fresh parsley

A salad that never fails to deliver – great for barbecues, parties or for a quick lunchtime snack. I like to serve my potatoes warm as it helps to lift the simple dressing to new heights.

METHOD

Cook the new potatoes in a saucepan of boiling water until tender but still firm, drain and set aside. Heat a frying pan over a medium heat, add the bacon and cook for about 6 minutes, stirring frequently, until the bacon is brown and crisp. Drain on kitchen paper.

Meanwhile whisk together the oil, vinegar and chilli with a pinch of salt and black pepper.

Trim and slice the spring onions on an angle about 2 cm (¾ in) long then slice the now warm but easy-to-handle new potatoes into rounds about 5 mm (¼ in) thick.

Arrange the potatoes on 4 plates in the shape of a flower. Sprinkle the bacon on top followed by the spring onions. Dribble over the dressing. Add a touch of chopped parsley and serve immediately.

NON-VULGAR BULGAR CHICKEN SALAD

SERVES 4 AS A STARTER OR 2 AS A MAIN COURSE

1 tablespoon mango chutney

1 tablespoon mixed curry paste

1 teaspoon ground turmeric

7 tablespoons olive oil

2 skinless chicken breasts, cut into strips about 3 × 1 cm (1¼ × ½ in) in size

1½ tablespoons white wine vinegar

75 g (3 oz) bulgar wheat

100 ml (3½ fl oz) boiling water

75 g (3 oz) cherry tomatoes, halved

4 spring onions, trimmed and chopped

1 tablespoon chopped fresh flat parsley

sprigs of parsley, to garnish

salt and freshly ground black pepper

This is one of those dishes that is so full of flavour that it has a really healthy bite to it. You can use turkey instead of chicken. If you use the grilling method, cover the grill tray with foil to catch and reserve the juices.

METHOD

Mix together the mango chutney, curry paste, turmeric and 4 tablespoons of the olive oil. Add the chicken, mix well and marinate for 30 minutes or more.

Cook the chicken either by frying it in the remaining oil over a high heat for 8–10 minutes or by grilling. This way will take a little longer, 10–12 minutes, but remember to keep the chicken in a single layer for a nice even brown colour, turning it occasionally.

When cooked transfer the chicken to a bowl along with the cooking juices. Add the vinegar, give a quick mix then cool. Place the bulgar wheat in a bowl and pour over the boiling water. Leave to soak for 8–10 minutes until the water is absorbed. Mix the bulgar wheat with the chicken, add the tomatoes, spring onions, parsley and season well. Garnish with sprigs of parsley.

CANNES CANNES
SALMON SALAD

SERVES 4 AS A STARTER OR 2 AS A MAIN COURSE

350 g (12 oz) fresh salmon

150 g (5 oz) fennel

½ cucumber, peeled, halved and seeded, and cut into 1 cm (½ inch) cubes

1 spring onion, trimmed and chopped

slices of lemon and lime, to garnish

VINAIGRETTE DRESSING:

juice and rind of 1 lemon

juice and rind of 1 lime

6 tablespoons olive oil

1 red chilli pepper, seeded and finely chopped

1 tablespoon roughly chopped fresh coriander

salt and freshly ground black pepper

first tasted this salad whilst I was on holiday in the South of France. I also remember drinking lots of bubbly stuff and doing the can can around the streets of Cannes. Ask your fishmonger for salmon tail which is cheaper. Use unwaxed lemons and limes if possible.

METHOD

First make the dressing. Whisk the lemon and lime rinds and juices together with the olive oil. Add the chilli, coriander and seasoning, and whisk again.

Poach the salmon in water for about 12 minutes. Drain and flake the fish, removing any bones.

Trim the fennel, reserving the leaves and slice the bulb finely. In a large bowl lightly mix the flaked fish with the cucumber, fennel slices and spring onion, then quickly stir in the vinaigrette. Do not over mix or stir as you will break up the salmon too much.

Garnish with the green leaves from the top of the fennel and twisted slices of lemon and lime. Serve with fresh granary bread.

PINEAPPLE, PEPPER AND PRAWN SALAD

1 medium-sized pineapple

4–5 tablespoons mayonnaise

1 teaspoon mild curry paste

225 g (8 oz) cooked, peeled prawns

2 small peppers (1 red and 1 green), seeded and cut into matchsticks

1 tablespoon grated fresh coconut (optional)

salt and freshly ground black pepper

50 g (2 oz) toasted flaked almonds

pinch of chilli powder or cayenne pepper

I made this dish on *Good Morning Summer* adorned in a Carmen Miranda fruit hat and dancing to 'Pineapple Princess'. It certainly had a lot of viewers laughing, judging by the letters and calls received.

Fresh pineapple is full of vitamins A and C and the enzymes in it are great for burning off the calories. For that extra special meal use large Mediterranean prawns. This is lovely as a light lunch or supper.

METHOD

Halve the pineapple lengthways, and cut out the flesh to leave 2 empty shells. Roughly chop the pineapple flesh into 2.5 cm (1 in) pieces and place in a bowl. Mix together the mayonnaise and the curry paste and add to the pineapple with the prawns, matchstick peppers and coconut (if using). Stir well, lightly season, stir again then place into the pineapple shells. Sprinkle the flaked almonds and chilli or cayenne on top and serve.

SOUPS

AUNTIE CYNTHIA'S CALLALOO SOUP **CLARE'S BEAN BROTH AND PESTO SOUP**

DELICIOUS PARSNIP SOUP **CHILLED SUMMER GAZPACHO SOUP** SMOKED

CAULIFLOWER CHEESE AND MUSTARD SOUP **AINSLEY'S CARIBBEAN COOK UP**

SOUP 'DOWN IN A FLASH' PUMPKIN AND POTATO SOUP

AUNTIE CYNTHIA'S CALLALOO SOUP

SERVES 4

50 g (2 oz) butter

6 slices of lean bacon, rinded and chopped

1 medium onion, peeled and chopped

1 red chilli pepper, de-seeded and sliced

2 cloves garlic, peeled and crushed

275 g (10 oz) callaloo or spinach leaves, washed and shredded

225 g (8 oz) unripe green banana, peeled and sliced

275 g (10 oz) potatoes, peeled and roughly chopped

½ teaspoon chopped fresh thyme or pinch of dried thyme

900 ml (1½ pints) chicken stock

600 ml (1 pint) coconut milk

225 g (8 oz) crabmeat (fresh, tinned or frozen)

salt and freshly ground black pepper

CORNMEAL SPINNERS:

110 g (4 oz) cornmeal

110 g (4 oz) plain flour

pinch of dried or chopped fresh thyme

½ teaspoon salt

water, to bind

Whilst filming for *Good Morning* in Trinidad I popped in to see my Auntie Cynthia and we cooked this delicious soup. It's more of a main course with all its hearty ingredients. You can replace the fresh or tinned callaloo (which is available in some supermarkets) with spinach or Swiss chord. Callaloo comes in two types, one with leaves shaped like small elephants' ears, the other similar to spinach or Indian kale. It is also known as dasheen – amongst other names – throughout the Caribbean. Cornmeal spinners are like dumplings.

METHOD

First make the cornmeal spinners. Mix all the dry ingredients together and add enough water to make a soft dough.

Melt the butter in a large saucepan over medium high heat without letting it brown. Add the bacon, onion, chilli and garlic, and stir fry for 2–3 minutes. Add the shredded callaloo or spinach and when cooked down by half, throw in the green banana, potatoes, thyme and chicken stock. Bring up to the boil then slowly pour and stir in the coconut milk. Reduce the heat, cover and simmer for 20 minutes.

Make the cornmeal spinners into finger-shaped pieces using floured hands then lower them into the simmering soup. Add the crabmeat and cook for a further 15 minutes. Taste and adjust the seasoning, then serve in warm bowls.

CLARE'S **BEAN BROTH** AND **PESTO SOUP** Ⓥ

SERVES 4

2 tablespoons olive oil

2 leeks, trimmed and cut into 2 cm (1 in) chunks

275 g (10 oz) potato, peeled and diced

1.75 litres (3 pints) light vegetable stock

175 g (6 oz) dwarf beans, cut into 2.5 cm (1 in) lengths

175 g (6 oz) runner beans, cut on an angle into 2.5 cm (1 in) lengths

1 × 275 g (10 oz) tin of broad beans, drained

1 × 275 g (10 oz) tin haricot beans, drained

225 g (8 oz) courgettes, diced

1 × 200 g (7 oz) tin chopped tomatoes

salt and freshly ground black pepper

2 tablespoons chopped fresh parsley

FOR THE PESTO:

3 cloves garlic

4–6 leafy stems of fresh basil

50 g (2 oz) pine nuts

50 g (2 oz) grated Parmesan

120 ml (4 fl oz) olive oil

Bean cookery has developed tremendously in recent years and now that supermarkets stock a wide range of beans in tins, you have the choice of using either dried or tinned. Tinned varieties are slightly more expensive but time saving and no hassle with preparation. If you use dried, always soak them well, preferably overnight, then rinse thoroughly before use to avoid windy situations!! You can use a jar of pesto but my fresh version is really quite superb.

METHOD

First make the pesto. Crush the garlic in a mortar or use a food grinder. Add the basil leaves and pine nuts and pound or blitz until it becomes a paste, then stir in the Parmesan and olive oil and set aside.

Heat the oil in a saucepan. Add the leeks and potatoes and fry without letting them colour for 2–3 minutes. Add the stock, bring to the boil, then cover and simmer for 20 minutes. Now add all the beans, the courgettes, tomatoes and simmer for a further 10–15 minutes. Taste and adjust the seasoning, and add the chopped parsley. Serve with a spoonful of the pesto stirred into each bowlful. Hot summer fun?

DELICIOUS PARSNIP **SOUP**

SERVES 4
25 g (1 oz) butter
450 g (1 lb) parsnips, peeled and chopped
1 medium onion, peeled and chopped
1 carrot, peeled and chopped
175 g (6 oz) potato, peeled and chopped
1 bay leaf
600 ml (1 pint) light vegetable stock
300 ml (½ pint) milk
¼ teaspoon cumin powder
salt and freshly ground black pepper
40 g (1½ oz) packet plain crisps, crushed
1 teaspoon chopped fresh chives

Parsnips make the perfect soup what with their delicate smell and sweetness, and rich creamy colour. I think you get the hint. Definitely one of my favourites.

METHOD

Melt the butter in a saucepan. Add the vegetables and the bay leaf and fry for 10 minutes without browning. Pour in the stock and milk, bring up to the boil then reduce the heat, cover and simmer for 30 minutes.

Remove the bay leaf and liquidize the soup. Return to a clear pan, taste and adjust the seasoning with cumin, salt and pepper. Serve in warm bowls with crushed crisps and chopped chives floating on the top.

CHILLED **SUMMER GAZPACHO** SOUP

SERVES 4-6

1 large red onion

1 large clove garlic

½ red pepper, seeded

½ green pepper, seeded

½ cucumber, peeled

3 thick slices of white bread, crusts removed

25 ml (1 fl oz) warm water

4 tablespoons virgin olive oil

2 tablespoons white wine vinegar

1 tablespoon raw cane sugar

1 teaspoon paprika

900 ml (1½ pints) tomato juice

325 ml (11 fl oz) vegetable juice

salt and freshly ground black pepper

TO GARNISH:

½ green pepper, seeded and diced

½ red pepper, seeded and diced

½ cucumber, skinned, halved seeded and diced

75 g (3 oz) white bread croûtons

A wonderful classic Spanish soup. Everybody likes to add their own personal touches and mine are paprika and sugar. Best to use a food processor for grating and blitzing. Alternatively, use a medium cheese grater for the onion and cucumber, crush the garlic and finely chop the peppers. I know this sounds like the method, but believe me it's the introduction.

METHOD

Peel and grate the onion, garlic, peppers and cucumber in the food processor, if using (see introduction). Place in a bowl and chill. Add the blade attachment to the food processor (no need to wash the bowl). Break the bread up into the bowl. Add the warm water and blitz, followed by the oil, vinegar, sugar and paprika, and blitz again.

Mix with the bowl of grated vegetables then stir in the tomato and vegetable juice. Season to taste with salt and pepper, stir in a tray of ice cubes and chill until needed.

Serve with individual bowls filled with the finely diced garnishes.

SMOKED **CAULIFLOWER CHEESE** AND **MUSTARD SOUP** ⓥ

SERVES 6

75 g (3oz) butter

100 g (4oz) onion, peeled and sliced

1 clove garlic, peeled and crushed

450 g (1 lb) cauliflower, roughly chopped small chunks

50 g (2 oz) plain flour

1.5 litres (2½ pints) chicken stock

100 g (4 oz) smoked cheese, grated

1 tablespoon wholegrain mustard

1 pinch of freshly grated nutmeg

salt and freshly ground black pepper

TO GARNISH:

120 ml (4 fl oz) double cream

Snipped fresh chives

Cauliflower can often be a bland vegetable, but here I've added smoked cheese and hot mustard to give it some zing. This soup can make a satisfying but light meal. Serve with hot crusty bread.

METHOD

Melt the butter in a heavy-based pan, add the onion and garlic and fry for 30 seconds. Add the cauliflower and gently fry until golden brown. Stir in the flour and cook for a further minute. Pour in the stock, gradually, stirring continuously until smooth. Cook for a further 15–20 minutes until the cauliflower is soft. Leave to cool slightly, then whizz in a blender or liquidizer until smooth. Pass the soup through a sieve and return to a clean pan. Stir in the cheese and mustard and warm gently over a low heat. Add a sprinkling of nutmeg, season to taste with salt and pepper and serve in warm serving bowls. Garnish with a swirl of double cream and scatter a few snipped chives on top.

AINSLEY'S CARIBBEAN **COOK UP** SOUP

SERVES 4

450 g (1 lb) chicken wings

50 ml (2 fl oz) vegetable oil

450 g (1 lb) shin of beef, cut into cubes and seasoned

1 large onion, peeled and sliced

2 cloves garlic, peeled and crushed

275 g (10 oz) yam, peeled

1 chilli pepper, seeded and chopped

¼ teaspoon dried thyme

450 g (1 lb) sweet potato, washed and roughly diced

1 × 400 g (14 oz) tin red kidney beans

1 × 225 g (8 oz) tin chopped tomatoes

5 cm (2 in) cinnamon stick

1.75 litres (3 pints) beef stock (use cubes)

salt and freshly ground black pepper

Sprigs of fresh thyme, to garnish

DUMPLINGS:

350 g (12 oz) plain flour

100 g (4 oz) cornmeal

½ teaspoon salt

water, to bind

This one is like a lot of traditional soups throughout the world – anything that's around in the larder gets thrown in! Yet it looks so controlled and tastes great. Pork can replace the beef and if you like food hot use extra chillies.

METHOD

Chop off the pointed top half of the chicken wings, then cut in half across the bone. Heat the oil in a large saucepan and fry the seasoned wings and beef until browned. Add the onion, garlic, yam, chilli, thyme and sweet potato. When the onion starts to get soft add the kidney beans, tomatoes, cinnamon stick and pour in the beef stock. Bring to the boil then cover and simmer for about 1 hour.

Meanwhile, make the dumplings. Mix all the dry ingredients together and add enough water to make a soft dough. Shape into balls about the size of whole walnuts using floured hands then lower them into the soup. Cook for a further 15–20 minutes until the dumplings are cooked through. Taste and adjust the seasoning. Garnish with sprigs of fresh thyme.

'DOWN IN A FLASH' PUMPKIN AND **POTATO SOUP** Ⓥ

SERVES 4-6

50 g (2 oz) butter

3 cloves garlic, peeled and crushed

2 medium onions, peeled and sliced

1 tablespoon medium strength curry powder

750 g (1½ lb) pumpkin, peeled, seeded and cut into 2.5 cm (1 in) cubes

750 g (1½ lb) potatoes, peeled and cut into 2.5 cm (1 in) cubes

1 × 400g (14 oz) tin chopped tomatoes

2 tablespoons chopped fresh coriander

½ teaspoon cayenne pepper

250 ml (8 fl oz) coconut milk

1.2 litres (2 pints) vegetable stock

salt and freshly ground black pepper

pinch of nutmeg

1 × 150 ml (5 fl oz) carton natural yoghurt (optional)

Every time I serve this soup, the bowls are left so clean my dishwasher thinks it's on holiday! Talk about `save on the suds'! If you've never tried pumpkin before, this is a great recipe to introduce yourself to it. Go on, be a devil.

METHOD

Melt the butter in a large saucepan, then fry the garlic and onions for 1 minute without letting them colour. Add the curry powder and stir for 30 seconds, then add the cubed pumpkin and potatoes. Continue to fry and stir for approx 5 minutes. Now add the tomatoes, coriander, cayenne pepper and then stir in the coconut milk and vegetable stock. Bring to the boil, cover and simmer for 35–40 minutes. Remove from the heat and cool slightly.

Liquidize the soup then return to a clean pan for reheating. If you like your soups chunky, like me, use a potato masher to break up some of the pieces instead of liquidizing. Season with salt, pepper and nutmeg and serve with a dollop of natural yoghurt if liked.

STARTERS

DENZIL'S HAM AND LEEK FILO TARTS **HOT QUACA MUSHROOMS** CRAB CRUNCH ROLLS WITH MANGO CHUTNEY **YAM AND SWEET POTATO SPLASH** GRILLED GARLIC CIABATTA WITH HERBY MOZZARELLA **WICKED AUBERGINE PÂTÉ** SWEET JEMIMA'S MUSHROOM PÂTÉ **WARM ASPARAGUS WITH LEMON BUTTER AND PARMESAN FLAKES** SPICY BEAN AND PLANTAIN RINGS **L'UOVO ORNOLDO BENNETTO** CREAMY SMOKED HADDOCK AND CRACKED PEPPER WITH PLANTAIN TWIRLS

DENZIL'S HAM AND LEEK FILO TARTS

SERVES 4 AS A STARTER OR LIGHT SUPPER

4 sheets filo pastry, defrosted if frozen

75 g (3 oz) butter

1 clove garlic, peeled and crushed

225 g (8 oz) leeks, trimmed and finely sliced

100 g (4 oz) honey-baked ham, diced

1 teaspoon chopped fresh coriander

pinch of freshly grated nutmeg

salt and freshly ground black pepper

50 g (2 oz) mixed lettuce leaves

4 tablespoons crème fraîche

cayenne pepper, for dusting

eeks are a wonderfully versatile vegetable – easy to cook and full of flavour. With the help of a few herbs, spices and some honey-baked ham, this simple recipe really comes alive. If you've not got a flan ring with a loose base, use a sealed one but be careful when removing the pastry cases. A small palette knife slid around the edge helps.

METHOD

Pre-heat the oven to gas mark 6, 400°F, 200°C. Carefully cut each sheet of filo pastry into four equal squares with a sharp knife. Melt 50 g (2 oz) of the butter and use a little to lightly brush 4 x 10 cm (4 in) round flan rings with removable bases. Line each flan ring with a square of filo and brush with a little melted butter. Repeat this process three times, layering each square at a different angle to make a star-shaped edge. Place the flan rings on a baking sheet and bake for 10 minutes until golden brown.

Heat the remaining butter in a frying pan or wok. Add the garlic and fry for a few seconds without allowing it to colour, then add the leeks and cook for 1–2 minutes, stirring. Add the diced ham and fresh coriander and toss until just heated through. Add nutmeg and season to taste.

To serve, line each plate with a selection of mixed lettuce leaves and place a filo tart on top. Spoon the leek mixture into each tart, top with a dollop of crème fraîche and dust with a little cayenne pepper. Serve while still warm.

HOT QUACA MUSHROOMS

2–3 rashers smoked streaky or back bacon

4 large flat mushrooms

salt and freshly ground black pepper

2 tablespoons olive oil

175 g (6 oz) cream cheese

1 tablespoon lemon juice

1 clove garlic, peeled and crushed

1 large ripe avocado

1 Caribe chilli pepper, seeded and finely chopped

1 large tomato, skinned, seeded and diced

50 g (2 oz) white breadcrumbs

50 g (2 oz) fresh Parmesan, finely grated

2 bunches fresh watercress, to serve

I don't know about you, but when I make avocado quacamole for a party I always seem to have some left over. I'm usually bored with using it as a dip by that stage, so here is a rather scrumptious way of using it up. Caribe chilli peppers are a yellow-green colour with a slightly sweet taste. If they are not available, use an ordinary chilli pepper but remember this will be hotter. Otherwise a tablespoon of chopped pimiento will do.

METHOD

Grill the bacon until crisp and set aside. Pre-heat the oven to gas mark 7, 425°F, 220°C. Remove the stalks from the mushrooms, chop finely and place on top of caps. Season the mushrooms and drizzle a teaspoon of the olive oil over each one. Pop onto a baking tray and put in the oven for 3–4 minutes. Remove and set on one side.

Put the cream cheese, lemon juice and garlic into a food processor and blitz for 10–15 seconds until fairly smooth. Cut the avocado into quarters, remove the skin and stone, roughly chop and add to the cream cheese mixture. Blitz again for another 10 seconds. Then scoop out into a bowl. Chop the bacon into small pieces, add to the quaca mixture, along with the chilli and diced tomato and mix together using a wooden spoon. Correct the seasoning.

Divide the quaca mixture equally onto the mushrooms. Mix together the breadcrumbs and the Parmesan, and sprinkle over the mushrooms. Drizzle a teaspoon of olive oil over each one and add a twist of black pepper. Put under a medium hot grill until crunchy brown. Serve on a bed of watercress.

CRAB CRUNCH ROLLS WITH MANGO CHUTNEY

SERVES 4

75 g (3 oz) unsalted butter

1 spring onion, trimmed and finely chopped

1 teaspoon grated root ginger

100 g (4 oz) white breadcrumbs

225 g (8 oz) white crab meat (fresh, tinned or frozen), well drained

1 teaspoon soy sauce

½ teaspoon piri piri seasoning

salt and freshly ground black pepper

4 whole iceberg lettuce leaves (unbroken)

mango chutney

1 fresh lime, quartered

Simple recipes are often the most enjoyable and this one certainly falls into that category. It's fresh and crunchy with a sweet zing which – dare I say it – is finger lickin' good. Piri piri seasoning is a Portuguese-style blend of crushed chillies and fragrant herbs which is available in supermarkets and delis in the spice section.

METHOD

Melt the butter in a large frying pan, add the spring onion and ginger and lightly fry for 30 seconds without letting them colour. Add the breadcrumbs and lightly fry until slightly golden brown. Now add the crab meat, soy sauce and piri piri. Mix well and correct the seasoning. When thoroughly heated, remove from the heat.

Lay out the lettuce leaves on a flat surface, place the crab mixture one third of the way down each leaf. Roll the lettuce over the top of the mixture and fold it in at the sides. Continue to roll until you have a large sausage. Serve immediately on a plate with a good dollop of mango chutney and a wedge of fresh lime.

YAM AND **SWEET POTATO** SPLASH

SERVES 6

1 kg (2 lb) yellow yams

450 g (1 lb) sweet potato

1 onion, peeled and finely chopped

2 egg yolks

75 g (3 oz) butter

1 tablespoon chopped fresh coriander

salt and freshly ground black pepper

75 g (3 oz) plain flour

1 egg, lightly beaten

450 g (1 lb) breadcrumbs

oil for deep frying

Sweet potato is very different to the potatoes that we know, but is equally versatile. They can be white, pink or purple and the flesh is creamy white or orange, yet all of them are tender and sweet when cooked. Yam is another root vegetable but one with a tough skin. The flesh can be white, yellow and purple. For this recipe, ask your greengrocer for yellow yams – although you could use white – since they present so much better.

METHOD

Peel and wash the yams and sweet potato. Cut into large, equal pieces and put into a saucepan of boiling salted water, and cook until tender (just like ordinary boiled potatoes). Drain well then mash adding the onion, egg yolks, butter, coriander and seasoning. Allow to cool slightly. Using the flour, shape the mixture into balls, and dip in first the egg and then the breadcrumbs. Deep fry in hot oil until golden brown. Drain and serve. Mango chutney is a nice accompaniment.

GRILLED GARLIC CIABATTA WITH HERBY MOZZARELLA Ⓥ

SERVES 4

50 g (2 oz) butter, softened

½ teaspoon rock salt

1 teaspoon Worcestershire sauce

2 plump cloves garlic, peeled and crushed

freshly ground black pepper

1 loaf ciabatta bread, cut in half lengthways

10 large basil leaves

3 × 150 g (5 oz) packets Mozzarella, cut into 12–14 slices

1 tablespoon chopped mixed herbs (e.g. parsley, sage and thyme)

a little olive oil (optional)

sprigs of fresh watercress

Did you know that Mozzarella is made from buffalo milk (although there are alternatives which come from the cow)? People are still astonished when I tell them. Yet it is becoming one of the most popular cooking cheeses in its class. Eat it cold in salads or hot with pastas, meat dishes or on crispy ciabatta bread like this…

METHOD

Pre-heat the grill until medium hot. Mix the butter, salt, Worcestershire sauce, garlic and 4–5 twists of pepper together. Spread over the ciabatta and place under the grill for about 4–5 minutes until lightly golden.

Remove from grill then lay 5 leaves of basil on top of each slice and 6–7 slices of Mozzarella. Sprinkle the mixed herbs on top then place back under the grill again until bubbling golden brown.

Drizzle over a little olive oil. Cut into fingers and serve with sprigs of fresh watercress.

WICKED AUBERGINE **PÂTÉ**

SERVES 4

2 large aubergines

1 clove garlic, peeled and crushed

1 small green chilli pepper, seeded and finely chopped

2 teaspoons lemon juice

2 tablespoons olive oil

salt and freshly ground black pepper

2 tablespoons chopped fresh parsley

TO GARNISH:

chopped fresh parsley

lemon wedges

This is one of my wife's favourite pâtés and is always made to titillate our friends' taste buds before the grand slam main course.

METHOD

Pre-heat the oven to gas mark 5, 375°F, 190°C. Prick the aubergines all over with a fork, cut in half and place them cut side down on a lightly greased baking sheet. Bake in the oven for 30–40 minutes until softened.

Scoop out the flesh then blitz in a food processor with the garlic, chilli and lemon juice, adding the olive oil one teaspoon at a time. Alternatively, chop the flesh of the aubergine finely and rub through a sieve, then crush the chilli and garlic in a pestle and mortar and add to the sieved aubergine with the lemon juice. Beat well then slowly mix in the olive oil in a steady stream until smooth.

Season with salt and pepper to taste and stir in the parsley. Spoon onto plates or serve in ramekin dishes. Garnish with parsley and lemon wedges and serve with crispy toast rubbed with garlic and olive oil.

OPPOSITE (clockwise from back left): *Pineapple, Pepper and Prawn Salad* (page 17); *Ainsley's Warm Winter Salad* (page 11) and *Non-vulgar Bulgar Chicken Salad* (Page 15)

SWEET JEMIMA'S MUSHROOM PÂTÉ Ⓥ

50 g (2 oz) butter
1 small onion, peeled and chopped
1 clove garlic, peeled and crushed
275 g (10 oz) flat mushrooms, wiped and sliced
1 tablespoon sherry (optional)
1 tablespoon lime juice
75 g (3 oz) fresh white breadcrumbs
100 g (4 oz) cream cheese
8 basil leaves, roughly torn
pinch of cayenne
salt and freshly ground black pepper

Pâtés normally hang around in the fridge just looking at you, but this one gets the 'See me, eat me' approval. Wait till you taste it. It's named after a girlfriend I once had.

METHOD

Melt the butter in a saucepan. Add the onion and garlic and cook for 2–3 minutes without letting it colour (remember the sweet smell that they release). Add the mushrooms and cook for 5 minutes on low to medium heat. If using the sherry add it now and increase the heat for 30 seconds. Take off the heat and cool slightly.

Put the mixture into a food processor with all the juices. Add the lime juice, breadcrumbs, cream cheese, basil, cayenne pepper, salt and pepper, and blitz until well combined. Taste and adjust the seasoning if necessary. Chill and serve with wholemeal toast and lime wedges.

OPPOSITE (clockwise from back left): *Clare's Bean Broth and Pesto Soup* (page 20); *Creamy Smoked Haddock and Cracked Pepper with Plantain Twirls* (page 37) and *Glazed Chicken Goujons with Hogincor Dressing* (page 52)

WARM ASPARAGUS WITH LEMON BUTTER AND PARMESAN FLAKES

SERVES 4

450 g (1 lb) bunch of asparagus

3 tablespoons white wine

100 g (4 oz) unsalted butter, softened

1 lemon, juiced and zested

salt and freshly ground black pepper

25 g (1 oz) fresh Parmesan, flaked

Asparagus is known as the aristocrat of vegetables. The English asparagus season traditionally starts on 1 May, but lasts only 6–8 weeks. It is deemed as a luxury, but when in season it gets quite cheap. Wild asparagus, known as sprue, is the thinner and cheaper variety. By flakes of Parmesan I mean grated on the area of the grater with the long blades, or peeled with a potato peeler. Only use the yellow lemon zest, not the white pith as it is bitter.

METHOD

Cook the asparagus in a pan of boiling water for 8–10 minutes until tender. Drain well and keep warm.

Heat the white wine in a pan and when it starts to boil whisk in the softened butter over a low heat until you have a double cream consistency, then add the lemon juice and zest. Taste and adjust the seasoning.

Lay the asparagus on 4 plates. Pour over the lemon butter and sprinkle with flakes of Parmesan. Add another twist or two of black pepper.

SPICY BEAN AND PLANTAIN RINGS

SERVES 4

2 large ripe plantains, each peeled and cut into 6 long strips lengthways

75 g (3 oz) butter

2 cloves garlic, peeled and crushed

2 spring onions, peeled and finely chopped

3 smoked back bacon rashers, rinded and cut into strips

1 tablespoon chopped fresh thyme

½ teaspoon cayenne pepper

350 g (12 oz) long-grain rice

1 × 425 g (15 oz) tin kidney beans

1 tablespoon tomato purée

75 g (3 oz) creamed coconut, grated

400 ml (14 fl oz) chicken stock

4 cocktail sticks

3 whole tomatoes, sliced

100 g (4 oz) cheese, grated (Cheddar and Edam work well)

Plantain is the largest of the banana family and for this dish the ideal plantain should be firm, but not over-ripe. Even though it is now widely available throughout Britain, TV presenter, Nick Owen hadn't tasted plantain until he tried this. Be careful when cutting the plantain. It may be a good idea after the first cut to lay it on the flat side for more control. Twelve slices allows three for each ring.

METHOD

Slice the plantains lengthways, about a quarter of an inch thick. Heat half the butter in a frying pan, add the plantain strips and fry for about 5 minutes, turning once, until they turn a rich golden brown colour. Drain on a piece of kitchen paper and set aside. Melt the remaining butter in a saucepan and add the garlic, spring onions and bacon and fry for about 1–2 minutes. Now add the thyme, cayenne pepper, rice, kidney beans, tomato purée and grated coconut. Stir well and when it starts to sizzle, add the chicken stock, bring to the boil then reduce the heat, cover and simmer for about 15–20 minutes, until the stock has been absorbed and the rice grains are tender.

Roll each slice of plantain into a ring and secure with a cocktail stick. Place on a sheet of foil then fill the centre with the rice mixture. Arrange slices of tomato on top, followed by a good sprinkling of grated cheese. Place under a medium grill until the cheese is melted and golden. Serve with a tossed mixed salad or hot savoy cabbage mixed with cream and crushed garlic.

L'UOVO ORNOLDO BENNETTO

SERVES 2

225 g (8 oz) smoked haddock

4 tablespoons double cream or crème fraîche

pinch of cayenne pepper

4 large eggs

1 tablespoon water

salt and freshly ground black pepper

25 g (1 oz) butter

2 tablespoons Parmesan (optional)

TO GARNISH:

3 tomatoes, sliced

1 tablespoon snipped chives

T hought I'd give you (unless you're Italian) a quick culinary Italian lesson. Translated it means 'omelette Arnold Bennett,' but that doesn't sound half as sexy.

The word omelette comes from the French word, *lamette*, which means small blade. This is because of the flat shape of the omelette. Make sure you use a good pan, preferably non-stick. For added zing replace the water with balsamic vinegar. Also you could replace the haddock and cream with grated cheese and chopped tomatoes, or fried mushrooms and fresh herbs.

METHOD

Poach the haddock in water or half milk and water (just enough liquid to cover the fish) for 8–10 minutes. Drain, remove the skin and any bones, and flake into a bowl. Stir in the cream or crème fraîche and a pinch of cayenne pepper.

Beat the eggs with the water, and add salt and pepper. Heat a non-stick frying pan and drop in the butter which will melt immediately, then pour in the egg mixture. Using a fork or spatula pull the sides in towards the middle, keeping the pan moving. When it starts to set, yet is still a little wet, pour the fish mixture on top. If using the Parmesan sprinkle it over now and place under a hot grill until lightly golden brown.

Slide the omelette onto a plate, garnish with a few slices of tomato around the side of the omelette and sprinkle chives over the tomatoes.

CREAMY SMOKED **HADDOCK** AND CRACKED **PEPPER** WITH **PLANTAIN TWIRLS**

SERVES 4

350 g (12 oz) smoked haddock

milk or milk and water for poaching

1 bay leaf

1 × 150 ml (5 fl oz) carton crème fraîche

1 chilli pepper, finely chopped

1 tablesppon black peppercorns, cracked

juice of 1 lime

pinch salt

1–2 large plantains

50–75 g (1–2 oz) butter

TO GARNISH:

sprigs of fresh flat parsley

red and yellow cherry tomatoes

I've used smoked haddock several times in this book so you'll probably know it's one of my favourites. However smoked cod is a good alternative. The blend of smoked haddock and plantain is a real winner.

Crack the peppercorns inside a sheet of clingfilm using a rolling pin or the base of a heavy pan.

METHOD

Poach the haddock in milk (just enough liquid to cover the fish) with the bay leaf. You could use half milk and half water. Cook for about 8–10 minutes, depending on the thickness and then remove from the pan. Meanwhile, pre-heat the oven to gas mark 4, 350°F, 180°C.

Once cooked, skin and then flake the fish into a bowl, removing any fish bones. Add the crème fraîche, chopped chilli, cracked peppercorns, lime juice and salt. Mix together, place in four buttered ramekins and put in the oven to heat through.

Peel the plantains and slice lengthways (make the slices at least 13 cm (5 in) long). Heat the butter in a frying pan, add the plantains and fry for about 5 minutes, turning once. They should be a rich golden brown colour. Drain on kitchen paper and immediately place 3 or 5 slices on a plate with the outside curled underneath to create a flower effect. Place the ramekin in the middle and garnish with flat parsley and, if you fancy, a few yellow and red cherry tomatoes.

FISH AND SEAFOOD

NO-CATCH FISHERMAN PIE **HALIBUT CRUSTED WITH HORSERADISH & HERBS**

SUPERB MACKEREL WITH CHILLI & HERBS **SALMON CREAM AND DOUBLE GREEN**

PRETTY PASSIONATE PAELLA **HIDDEN OATMEAL HERRING FILLETS WITH LIME**

AND PARSLEY BUTTER PORTUGUESE SWEET-PEPPERED PAN-FRIED COD

BARBECUED BREAM WITH SHRIMP AND CRAB, SERVED WITH COLUMBO SAUCE

GRILLED TUNA WITH GREEN LENTIL SALAD **HERBY HINTERZARTEN TROUT WITH**

ZESTY OYSTER MUSHROOMS

NO-CATCH FISHERMAN PIE

SERVES 4

750 g (1½ lb) fresh fish (e.g. cod, salmon, pollack, smoked haddock, monkfish)

milk and water for poaching

1 bay leaf

25 g (1 oz) butter

1 bulb fennel, trimmed and finely sliced

150 g (5 oz) button mushrooms

1 tablespoon brandy (optional)

120 ml (4 fl oz) dry white wine

1 × 400 g (14 oz) tin lobster or crab bisque soup

4 tablespoons double cream

1 tablespoon chopped dill

salt and freshly ground black pepper

175 g (6 oz) peeled prawns

3 hard-boiled eggs, shelled and cut into ½ moon shapes

1 kg (2 lb) cooked, mashed potato, mixed with 2 egg yolks

nutmeg

2 tablespoons milk

TO GARNISH:

Salad leaves

sprigs of fresh dill

Well . . . how many of us actually catch the fish we eat? Those of you who do will know the real beauty of catching fresh fish. Others, like me, rely on our fishmonger – most of the time. Get them to do any boning or cleaning for you and ask them to introduce you to new fish on the market. You'll need 3 or 4 varieties for this dish.

METHOD

Pre-heat the oven to gas mark 5, 375°F, 190°C.

Poach the fish (excluding prawns) in milk and water with the bay leaf. Drain, discarding the bay leaf and retaining 150 ml (5 fl oz) of the cooking liquor. Flake the fish into large pieces, removing the skin and bones. Heat the butter in a pan. Add the fennel and mushrooms and fry for 2–3 minutes. Add the brandy (if using) and, if you are feeling flamboyant, flambé to burn off the alcohol.

Add the white wine and reserved cooking liquor, bring to boil and reduce by half. Pour in the lobster soup and double cream. Stir and heat through, then stir in the dill, season with salt and pepper and remove from the heat. Put the fish in a pie dish, scatter over the prawns and egg then pour the sauce over the top. Cool slightly.

Meanwhile, season the mashed potato with salt, pepper and nutmeg, add the milk, beat well then pipe over the top of the pie. If you haven't got a piping bag, spoon the potato mixture over the top and spread roughly over the pie with a fork. Bake for 20–25 minutes until golden brown. Serve garnished with sprigs of dill. No catch? No matter – just enjoy!

HALIBUT CRUSTED WITH
HORSERADISH & HERBS

SERVES 4

75 g (3 oz) fresh white breadcrumbs

2 teaspoons snipped chives

2 teaspoons finely chopped dill

2 tablespoons olive oil

1 teaspoon grated horseradish

4 tinned anchovy fillets, drained and chopped

25 g (1 oz) butter, softened

4 × 175 g (6 oz) boneless halibut fillets

freshly ground black pepper

SAUCE:

150 ml (¼ pt) dry white wine

75 g (3 oz) butter (softened)

salt and freshly ground black pepper

1 teaspoon snipped fresh chives

Halibut is one of the most flavourful flat fishes. It's not too expensive, unlike turbot or brill, and it goes well with other ingredients. Anchovies and horseradish make it just that little bit more special. You can use horseradish relish as it is more widely available than fresh.

METHOD

Pre-heat the oven to gas mark 7, 425°F, 220°C.

Mix together the breadcrumbs, chives, dill, olive oil, horseradish and anchovies and set on one side. Rub the butter all over the fillets and season them. Bake in an ovenproof dish in the oven for about 4 minutes until about half cooked. Reduce the oven temperature to gas mark 6, 400°F, 200°C. Remove the fillets from the oven and spread the herb and breadcrumb mixture over them. Grind a little black pepper over the fillets, then return to the oven for about 5–6 minutes until golden.

To make the sauce, put the wine into a pan and reduce by half over a high heat. Then slowly whisk in the butter, season with salt and pepper and add the chives. Spoon the sauce onto four plates and top with the fillets. Serve with linguine pasta.

SUPERB MACKEREL WITH CHILLI & HERBS

SERVES 4

4 × 275g (10 oz) whole mackerel, gutted and cleaned

50g (2 oz) fresh mixed herbs (e.g. chives, chervil, dill, parsley and tarragon), chopped

2 red chilli peppers, seeded and finely chopped

1 tablespoon sesame oil

2 tablespoons olive oil

2 tablespoons soy sauce

salt and freshly ground black pepper

oil for frying

Mackerel is a firm favourite of mine. Packed full of vitamins A and D, it's excellent value for money and available all year round. For a healthy diet, oily fish should be eaten at least once a week.

METHOD

Make three 5 mm (¼ in) deep slashes across each fish, then repeat in the opposite direction. Reserve 15g (½ oz) of the herbs and smear the rest inside the fish. Transfer to a shallow dish. Mix together the reserved herbs, chilli, sesame and olive oils, soy sauce and salt and pepper. Spoon over the fish, working it into the grooves. Cover and chill for 2 hours.

Heat the oil in a large frying pan. Cook the fish on the uncut side for 4 minutes. Place under a medium grill, cut side up, for 4–6 minutes until crisp. Serve with *Coconut Rice* (page 103) and a nice salad of your choice.

SALMON CREAM AND DOUBLE GREEN

SERVES 4

1 bunch of watercress

50 g (2 oz) butter

2 shallots peeled and finely chopped

about 150 ml (¼ pint) dry white wine

300 ml (½ pint) double cream

salt and freshly ground black pepper

2 tablespoons olive oil, plus extra for brushing

4 × 175 g (6 oz) salmon fillets

450 g (1 lb) fresh spinach

a little freshly grated nutmeg

2 tomatoes, peeled, de-seeded and diced

boiled new potatoes, to serve

Salmon isn't one of my favourite fish, but I've brought a new dimension to it by serving it with creamy spinach and watercress.

METHOD

Remove the stalks from the watercress, roughly chop the leaves and set aside. Roughly chop the stalks and place in a pan with 25 g (1 oz) of the butter and the shallots. Cook over a medium heat for about 30–40 seconds, then increase the heat and add the wine. Reduce the liquid by half, then add the cream and reduce by half again. Strain the sauce, season with salt and pepper and keep it warm.

Heat the oil in a frying pan and season the salmon. Cook, skin side down, for about 4 minutes, then turn over and cook for a further 2 minutes. Remove the fish from the pan and keep it warm. Lightly steam the spinach for 2–3 minutes until it turns limp, then add the remaining butter and the nutmeg. Strain the sauce, return to the pan and adjust the seasoning. Place the spinach in the centre of four warm serving plates, pour around the cream sauce, sprinkle chopped watercress on top and diced tomato. Then place the salmon, skin side up, on top of the spinach, having rubbed a little olive oil on top for a glossy sheen. Serve with hot new potatoes.

PRETTY PASSIONATE PAELLA

SERVES 4–6

10–12 mussels

225 g (8 oz) cooked prawns

750 ml (1¼ pints) light chicken stock

1 bay leaf

4 tablespoons olive oil

450 g (1 lb) chicken cut into small pieces (not too much bone)

2 cloves garlic, peeled and chopped

1 onion, peeled and sliced

1 green pepper, de-seeded and sliced

1 red pepper, de-seeded and sliced

1 sprig of fresh rosemary

350 g (12 oz) long-grain rice

120 ml (4 fl oz) dry white wine

good pinch of saffron threads or 1 teaspoon turmeric

100 g (4 oz) chorizo sausage or kabanos (optional), sliced into 1 cm (½ in) rounds

1 x 200 g (7 oz) tin chopped tomatoes

salt and freshly ground black pepper

1–2 tablespoons roughly chopped fresh parsley

1 lemon, cut into wedges, to garnish

In Spain, this is cooked and served straight from a two-handled pan called a paella from which the dish takes its name. There are many variations depending on the region. Kabanos is a spicy sausage, like chorizo but thinner.

METHOD

Clean the mussels in a sink or bucketful of cold water, throwing out any that float to the top. Scrape off any barnacles and pull off the hairy beards. Discard only mussels that are open or damaged. When you've prepared all the mussels, give them several, brisk changes of cold water, and leave in the water until ready to cook them.

Peel the prawns keeping back 4 or 5 for the garnish. Put the peelings in a pan with the chicken stock, add the bay leaf and bring to the boil. Simmer for 5 minutes then strain, discarding the peelings and bay leaf. Heat the olive oil in the pan and brown the chicken for about 3–4 minutes then add the garlic, onion, peppers and rosemary and fry for 2–3 minutes. Add the rice and stir until coated in oil then add the white wine, saffron or turmeric, mussels, sausage and tomatoes. Stir and increase the heat, until bubbling, for about 1–2 minutes. Add the chicken stock and salt and pepper. Bring back to the boil and simmer partially covered for about 20–25 minutes until all the stock is absorbed. Different long-grain rices vary in how quickly they absorb the stock so keep an eye on the pan.

Remove the open mussels from the pan and discard half the shell. Discard any mussels which haven't opened completely. Serve garnished with lemon and sprinkled with parsley.

HIDDEN OATMEAL **HERRING** FILLETS WITH LIME AND **PARSLEY BUTTER**

75 g (3 oz) butter

rind and juice of ½ lime

1 tablespoon chopped fresh parsley

pinch of cayenne pepper

salt and freshly ground black pepper

2 large boneless herring fillets

50 g (2 oz) oatmeal

1 tablespoon olive oil

slices of lime (use remaining half), to garnish

Are you one of those people with a packet of oatmeal hidden in the back of your cupboard? Well, it's time to use it up and if you've never tried oatmeal on fish, it's a great new experience. Get the fishmonger to fillet the herring for you. The lime butter will keep for a couple of weeks in the fridge.

METHOD

Soften 50 g (2 oz) of the butter and mix in the lime rind and the juice, the parsley and cayenne. Cut off a piece of greaseproof paper, 20 cm (8 in) square. Using wet hands, shape the butter and lime mixture into a log shape on the paper. Then roll the paper around and twist the ends to form a cylinder shape. Chill in the freezer for 20 minutes or in fridge for a few hours before cutting.

Season with salt and pepper, then dip the herrings in oatmeal and fry in the oil and remaining butter for 2–3 minutes each side over a medium heat. Serve on a plate with slices of lime butter and lime on the top. *Dutch Capusanus Potatoes* (see page 91) go nicely with this.

PORTUGUESE **SWEET-PEPPERED** PAN-FRIED **COD**

2 × 175–225 g (6–8 oz) cod fillets

1 teaspoon piri piri seasoning

3 tablespoons olive oil

1 small red and green and yellow pepper, seeded and sliced

1 clove garlic peeled and crushed

1 teaspoon chopped fresh thyme

½ teaspoon fennel seeds

2 fl oz sherry

25 g (1 oz) butter

salt and freshly ground black pepper

All peppers start off green and gradually, with the right climate, they turn yellow and red. Mix the three together and the tricolour effect is visually brilliant, as this dish will show you. You can get piri piri seasoning in small jars at many supermarkets.

METHOD

Season the cod fillets with the piri piri on the flesh side. Drizzle 1 tablespoon of the olive oil over both sides of the fish then set aside. Heat 1 tablespoon of the olive oil in a frying pan. Add the peppers, garlic, thyme and fennel seeds and gently fry until the peppers have a light brown tinge on the edge. Pour on the sherry, flambé if you're feeling flamboyant, then cover and simmer over a low heat for 20–25 minutes, stirring occasionally. With about 15 minutes to go, heat the remaining oil and the butter and fry the cod for 4–5 minutes each side until golden brown. Taste and adjust the seasoning in the peppers. Serve the cod on top of the pepper mixture with crisp sautéed potatoes.

BARBECUED BREAM WITH SHRIMP AND CRAB, SERVED WITH COLUMBO SAUCE

SERVES 4–6

1.5–1.75 kg (3–4 lb) whole fish, boned and cleaned

STUFFING:

1 onion, peeled and finely chopped

1 red pepper, seeded and chopped

1 clove garlic, peeled and crushed

2.5 cm (1 in) root ginger, peeled and chopped

175 g (6 oz) cooked peeled prawns

175 g (6 oz) white crabmeat (fresh, frozen or tinned)

75 g (3 oz) white breadcrumbs

1 tablespoon chopped fresh coriander

120 ml (14 fl oz) dry white wine

½ teaspoon piri piri seasoning or cayenne pepper

4 tablespoons olive oil

salt and freshly ground black pepper

lemon wedges, to garnish

COLUMBO SAUCE:

2 tablespoons olive oil

1 onion, peeled and finely chopped

1 red chilli pepper, de-seeded and chopped

1 green pepper, finely diced

Another one of these dishes that cooks equally well in the oven or on the barbecue. I cooked mine on Belvoir beach on the island of Hern whilst the rest of the *Good Morning* team were celebrating 50 years since the liberation of the Channel Islands. If you can't get sea bream, use any large fish for stuffing such as pollack, sea bass or cod. Ask your fishmonger to bone out the fish from the belly so only one side is open for stuffing.

METHOD

Pre-heat the oven (if not using barbecue) to gas mark 7, 425°F, 220°C.

Take two large sheets of foil, place one on top of the other, brush with oil and lay your prepared fish on top. Mix together the stuffing ingredients using only 2 tablespoons of the olive oil which along with the wine will bind everything together. Use your hands to fill the inside of the fish with the stuffing. Brush the outside of the fish with the remaining oil then fold the foil loosely tucking in the top and ends to form a pillow. This allows steam to circulate around the fish. Put onto a hot barbecue or in the oven for 25–30 minutes. To check if it's cooked, open the foil at the top (be careful of the steam), and make a small cut into the fish. It should be creamy white, not silvery and raw.

Whilst cooking the fish make the columbo sauce. Heat the olive oil in a pan, add the onion and fry for 1 minute. Then add the chilli, pepper and celery, fry for another 2 minutes and add the

2 sticks celery, trimmed and finely diced

1 tablespoon chopped fresh mixed herbs (e.g. parsley, tarragon and basil)

25 ml (1 fl oz) dry white wine

1 × 400 g (14 oz) tin chopped tomatoes

1 tablespoon tomato purée

salt and freshly ground black pepper

herbs, white wine, tomatoes and tomato purée. Slowly bring to the boil then cover and simmer for 15–20 minutes. Taste and adjust the seasoning. Open the foil to reveal the fish inside. Place on an oval dish and present inside the foil with the sauce on the side. Garnish with lemon wedges. This goes really well with cheesey jacket potatoes. Cook them on the barbecue wrapped in foil for about 40–45 minutes or start them in the microwave for 10 minutes then wrap in foil and barbecue for a further 20 minutes.

GRILLED TUNA WITH GREEN LENTIL SALAD

SERVES 2

1 × 450 g (1lb) tin green lentils

2 plum tomatoes, finely chopped

50 g (2 oz) diced mixed peppers (red, green or yellow)

1 chilli pepper, finely chopped

1 spring onion, trimmed and finely chopped

2 tablespoons soy sauce

1 tablespoon white wine vinegar

3 tablespoons olive oil

1 tablespoon mixed chopped fresh herbs (e.g. coriander, basil and parsley)

salt and freshly ground black pepper

2 x 175 g (6 oz) fresh tuna fish steaks

Sprig of fresh coriander, to garnish

Tuna is the fillet steak of the fish world. It should be cooked lightly as overcooking will dry it out. You can even eat it slightly underdone. Don't be put off – remember sushi, the Japanese raw fish delicacy. Sword fish and salmon can also be used. If you prefer to use dried lentils, cook them in chicken stock with a few vegetables (e.g. carrots, celery, onion, garlic) and a bay leaf.

METHOD

Put the lentils into a saucepan and warm slightly. Remove from the heat and drain. (If using dried lentils, after cooking drain and remove the vegetables and bay leaf.) Place in a large bowl and then add the diced tomatoes, peppers, chilli and spring onion. Now add the soy sauce, vinegar, 2 tablespoons of the olive oil, and the fresh herbs. Season, mix well and set aside.

Heat a cast-iron ridged grill pan until hot. Season the tuna and brush with the remaining olive oil. Grill for 2–3 minutes on each side, depending on their thickness. Place a mound of lentil salad in the middle of a plate, carve the tuna steak at an angle and arrange on top of the salad with a sprig of fresh coriander.

HERBY **HINTERZARTEN TROUT** WITH **ZESTY OYSTER** MUSHROOMS

1 × 275 g (10 oz) fresh rainbow trout, gutted and cleaned

1 tablespoon chopped fresh mixed herbs (e.g. tarragon, dill, parsley and mint)

rind and juice of ½ lemon

2 tablespoons double cream

salt and freshly ground black pepper

2 tablespoons olive oil

25 g (1 oz) butter

75 g (3 oz) oyster mushrooms (cut in half, if large)

This dish comes fresh from the hills of the Hinterzarten in Germany. I caught the fish in the lake, picked the herbs from the surrounding countryside and cooked it for the chef at our hotel. He was most impressed. 'Das ist gut,' he said …

METHOD

Make three 5 mm (¼ in) slashes across the fish then repeat in the opposite direction. Mix the herbs with the lemon rind and rub half into the inside and slashed outside of the trout. Spoon the double cream into the slashed side allowing it to run over the trout. Season with salt and pepper.

Heat the olive oil in the frying pan and fry the fish slashed side first for 3–4 minutes on each side over a medium heat (be careful of any splashes). Remove from the pan, place on a plate and keep warm. Pour off any excess oil. Add the butter to the pan and when it starts to sizzle add the lemon juice, oyster mushrooms and the remaining herbs. Toss and fry until the mushrooms start to weep. Season, then splash over the top of the trout. Serve with *Creamy Garlic Potatoes* (see page 95).

POULTRY

CHICKEN SHOW STOPPER STIR-FRY **GLAZED CHICKEN GOUJONS WITH**

HOGINCOR DRESSING ROLL OVER CHILLI CREAM CHEESE GARLIC CHICKEN

CASHEW CALYPSO CHICKEN COR!! CORIANDER LEMON CHICKEN **CHICKEN, LEEK**

AND BACON RAP PIE CHICKEN BRUMMIE BALTI **TURKEY POCKETS WITH SPINACH**

AND CHEESE HAM & TURKEY IN THE HOLE WITH A CRISPY CRUNCHY TOPPING

GOLDEN TURKEY HOLSTEIN CHICKEN LIVERS AND SLIVERS OF GARLIC AND

WATER CHESTNUT ON CRISPY SEAWEED

CHICKEN SHOW STOPPER **STIR-FRY**

1 stick celery

1 carrot, peeled

½ red pepper

½ green pepper

1 small head broccoli

4 baby corn cobs

6 button mushrooms

2 plump boneless chicken breasts, cut into strips 1 cm (½ in) wide and 7.5 cm (3 in) long

2 tablespoons soy sauce

1 tablespoon sesame oil

2 tablespoons groundnut oil

3 spring onions, trimmed and sliced on an angle

1 clove garlic, peeled and chopped

2.5 cm (1 in) piece root ginger, peeled and finely chopped

75 g (3 oz) beanshoots

2 tablespoons clear honey

2 tablespoons hoisin sauce (Chinese barbecue sauce)

2 tablespoons water

freshly ground black pepper

I did this quick stir-fry live at the Ideal Home Exhibition in front of hundreds of onlookers. It was great fun especially at the end when I did a quick clothes change in front of camera then dashed to the other side of the exhibition hall to witness the wedding of the *Good Morning* couple of the year. Once you've got all your ingredients ready, this dish is prepared in minutes so cook your rice or noodles beforehand.

METHOD

Cut the celery, carrot, peppers, broccoli, corn cobs and mushrooms horizontally into slices or lengthways into batons. Mix the chicken with the soy sauce and sesame oil. Heat a wok or large frying pan and then put in the groundnut oil. Swirl around the wok so it is well coated then add the chicken and stir-fry for 2–3 minutes.

Remove with a slotted spoon and keep warm. Throw the spring onions, garlic and ginger into the wok and fry for 30 seconds then add the vegetables except the beanshoots and continue to stir-fry over a high heat until crisp and tender. Now add the beanshoots, chicken, honey, hoisin sauce and water. Toss, heat for 3–4 minutes, season with pepper and serve with steamed rice or noodles.

GLAZED CHICKEN GOUJONS WITH HOGINCOR DRESSING

SERVES 2 AS A MAIN COURSE OR 4 AS A STARTER

2 × 175–225 g (6–8 oz) boneless chicken breasts, skinned

450 ml (¾ pint) chicken stock

rind and juice of 1 lemon

4 tablespoons clear honey

1 tablespoon sesame seeds

3 plum tomatoes, sliced lengthwise

6 Chinese leaves, shredded

1 bunch watercress

DRESSING:

6 coriander seeds, crushed or ¼ teaspoon ground coriander

1 shallot, peeled and finely chopped

1 clove garlic peeled and crushed

2.5 cm (1 in) piece root ginger, peeled and grated or ½ teaspoon ground ginger

1 tablespoon soy sauce

120 ml (4 fl oz) dry white wine

2 tablespoons clear honey

1 tablespoon sesame oil

1 tablespoon chopped fresh coriander

TO GARNISH:

a few sprigs of fresh coriander

toasted sesame seeds

This dish looks so attractive when finished it's hard to stop yourself eating one of the chicken pieces. 'Hogincor' is another of my abbreviations – HOney, GINger, CORiander. The chicken stock that's left over after this recipe can be used in a soup or sauce.

METHOD

Poach the chicken breasts in the stock until tender (6–8 minutes). Cool, slice into thin strips and then set aside.

To make the dressing measure out 120 ml (4 fl oz) of the chicken stock into a pan and add the ground coriander, shallot, garlic, ginger, soy sauce, wine and honey. Bring to the boil, then simmer, uncovered, until reduced by half. Strain. Then, when slightly cool, whisk in the sesame oil and chopped fresh coriander. Set aside.

Heat the lemon juice, rind and honey in a saucepan until caramelized. Add the chicken strips and mix until well coated. Remove from the heat and stir in the sesame seeds. Mix until the chicken strips are again well coated.

Arrange the sliced tomatoes on the two plates.

Mix the watercress with the Chinese leaves (reserving a few sprigs of watercress for garnishing) and place a mound in the centre of the plate. Drizzle the dressing over and then place the chicken on top. Garnish with the remaining sprigs of watercress, fresh coriander and a little sprinkling of toasted sesame seeds.

ROLL OVER **CHILLI** CREAM **CHEESE** GARLIC **CHICKEN**

SERVES 4

4 flattened boneless breasts of chicken, including fillets
125 g (5 oz) cream cheese
2 cloves garlic, peeled and crushed
1 red chilli pepper, finely chopped
1 teaspoon snipped chives
salt and freshly ground black pepper
2 tablespoons olive oil
2 shallots, finely chopped
120 ml (4 fl oz) white wine
50 g (2 oz) butter, softened
½ tablespoon tomato purée
1 tablespoon chopped fresh basil
1 tomato, skinned, seeded and diced
snipped chives to garnish

A really nice chicken dish that goes down well on those special occasions. You can usually buy the flattened breast in your supermarket or get your butcher to do it for you.

METHOD

Lay the chicken on a flat surface without the fillet. Beat the cream cheese until smooth and add the garlic, chilli, chives and a touch of seasoning. Spread over the breasts leaving the edges clear. Lay the flattened fillet on top, then roll up starting with the pointed end and turning the edges in so the filling is sealed in when cooking.

Cut four pieces of foil about 15 cm (6 in) square. Brush with a little oil on the shiny side. Put the chicken sausages on top and roll the foil up tightly, twisting the ends firmly to form a tight cylinder. Place in a pan with enough boiling water to cover the sausages and poach for 15–20 minutes until cooked through. If you insert a skewer into the centre of the sausage it should be hot to touch when it is withdrawn. Switch off the heat and leave the sausages in the water whilst you make the sauce.

Put the shallots into a pan with the white wine. Bring to the boil and reduce by three quarters to leave a syrupy glaze. Whisk in the butter away from the heat to make a creamy consistency. Add the tomato purée, basil, diced tomato, and season to taste. Unwrap the foil from the chicken sausages and make one cut on an angle in each. Spoon a little sauce onto the centre of the plates and lay the chicken on top, slightly open to reveal the filling. Spoon over the remaining sauce and sprinkle with chives.

CASHEW CALYPSO CHICKEN

SERVES 4

3 tablespoons vegetable oil

2 tablespoons white wine vinegar

2 cloves garlic, peeled and crushed

rind and juice of 1 lime

½ teaspoon chopped fresh thyme, to garnish

1 tablespoon soy sauce

salt and freshly ground black pepper

4 boneless breasts of chicken

50 g (2 oz) butter

1 tablespoon brown sugar

100 g (4 oz) cashew nuts

2 medium onions, peeled and diced

5 cm (2 in) piece root ginger, peeled and finely chopped

175 g (6 oz) button mushrooms, sliced

300 ml (½ pint) chicken stock

1 teaspoon cornflour

1–2 tablespoons water

sprigs of fresh thyme, to garnish

I have fond memories of cooking this classic Jamaican dish with Maud, a lovely meals-on-wheels cook from Brixton. It was at the Dorchester in London doing a *Surprise Surprise* show with Cilla Black and Fern Britton. We had a fun time dancing around the kitchen under the watchful eye of the hotel's executive chef and his enormous brigade.

METHOD

Mix together 2 tablespoons of the vegetable oil, white wine vinegar, garlic, rind and juice of the lime, thyme and soy sauce. Season with salt and pepper. Cover the chicken breasts with this mixture and leave to marinate for 2–3 hours.

Melt the butter in a deep frying pan, add the sugar and when it starts to bubble add the chicken (reserving the leftover marinade) and fry for 3–4 minutes until browned. Remove from the pan. Add 75 g (3 oz) of the cashew nuts to the frying pan with the onions and ginger. Gently fry for 2 minutes then add the mushrooms. Fry for a further minute then pour in the stock and the reserved marinade. Bring up to boil and reduce by half. Slake the cornflour with 1–2 tablespoons water then stir into the mixture. Return the chicken to the pan, cover and simmer for 10 minutes. In a small pan lightly fry off the remaining cashew nuts in the remaining vegetable oil until golden brown. Taste and adjust the seasoning of the chicken sauce. Place the chicken and sauce in a pretty serving dish. Scatter the cashew nuts on top and garnish with sprigs of fresh thyme.

Serve with *Coconut Rice* (see page 103).

COR!! CORIANDER
LEMON **CHICKEN**

SERVES 4

1.5 kg (3 lb) chicken cut into 7.5 cm (3 in) pieces

salt and freshly ground black pepper

3 cloves garlic, peeled and chopped

2 tablespoon lemon juice

2 tablespoons ground coriander

50 g (2 oz) butter

2 tablespoons olive oil

TO GARNISH:

sprigs of fresh coriander or roughly chopped coriander

lemon wedges

Fresh coriander is a delightful addition to all kinds of sauces, relishes, soups and stuffings. Its strong, distinctive flavour livens up oriental cooking and has done for hundreds of years, so if you're a fan you'll love this recipe. You can use chicken legs, breasts or thighs – or a mixture – for this recipe.

METHOD

Pre-heat the oven to gas mark 5, 375°F/190°C. Season the chicken pieces with salt and pepper then rub in garlic, lemon juice, and ground coriander, then marinate for 2–3 hours or if you like, overnight.

Heat the butter and the oil in a frying pan and brown off the chicken over a high heat. You are only colouring it at this stage. Remove and put into an ovenproof dish, pour the butter and oil from the pan over the top then bake for about 1–1¼ hours until cooked through. If you require more browning on top pop it under the grill for a minute or two.

Serve garnished with sprigs of coriander or sprinkled with chopped coriander and lemon wedges. Great with basmati rice and a grated carrot, nut and sultana salad.

CHICKEN, LEEK AND
BACON RAP PIE

salt and freshly ground black pepper

1–1.25 kg (2–2½ lb) boneless chicken joints (use leg, breast and thigh)

12 rashers back or streaky bacon, rinded

600 ml (1 pint) chicken stock

2 bay leaves

½ teaspoon chopped fresh parsley

50 g (2 oz) butter

25 g (1 oz) plain flour

150 ml (5 fl oz) double cream

2–3 leeks, trimmed and sliced

350 g (12 oz) puff pastry

1 egg, lightly beaten with a tablespoon of water

Wrap that bacon round those thighs,
To make your chicken pie real nice,
Don't forget the legs and breast,
You've also got to please your guest,
A creamy sauce that's out of sight,
For an extra delicious succulent bite,
A pastry that is creamy rich,
That'll guarantee plates with nothing to ditch.

METHOD

Pre-heat the oven to gas mark 7, 425°F, 220°C. Season the chicken joints and wrap each piece with a rasher of bacon. Put in an ovenprooof dish in a single layer. Pour over 150 ml (5 fl oz) of the chicken stock, add the bay leaves and chopped parsley, then bake in the oven for 15 minutes. The stock keeps the chicken moist. Melt 25 g (1 oz) of the butter in a pan, add the flour, mix well then stir or whisk in the remaining stock, plus stock from around the chicken pieces and the cream. Season and cook out for 5 minutes then stir in the leeks. Pour over the chicken and cool. Reduce the oven temperature to gas mark 5, 375°F, 190°C.

On a floured surface, roll out the pastry large enough to cover the pie dish but not too thin. Butter the rim and line with pastry trimmings, then dampen the edges and cover the pie with pastry. Trim and seal the edges then decorate with pastry leaves and make a small slit in the top for steam to escape. Brush with egg wash, making sure you avoid the edges so it will rise evenly and bake in the oven for 20–25 minutes until well risen and golden brown.

CHICKEN BRUMMIE BALTI

SERVES 1-2

3 tablespoons vegetable oil

350 g (12 oz) boneless chicken meat, cut into mouthsized pieces

1 teaspoon turmeric

1 teaspoon cumin

1 teaspoon chilli powder

1 teaspoon paprika

salt

1 onion, peeled and chopped

2 cloves garlic, peeled and crushed

2.5 cm (1 in) piece root ginger, peeled and grated

½ green pepper, seeded and sliced

pinch of fenugreek (optional but wicked)

1 × 200 g (7 oz) tin chopped tomatoes

1 tablespoon tomato purée

3 tablespoons water

1 teaspoon chopped fresh coriander

TO GARNISH:

1 tomato

sprig of fresh coriander

Baltis are the latest fashion in food from the Indian subcontinent to hit the UK. They originate from Pakistan and have become one of Birmingham's most famous attractions. *Balti* actually means bucket and refers to the pot they are cooked in, which resembles a small wok. The essence of a good balti is its freshness and it can include any meat, fish, vegetables or pulses. Discard your knives and forks for this one: baltis are best eaten scooped up in a warm chapatti or naan bread. You can buy balti pots from good kitchen shops.

METHOD

Heat 1½ tablespoons of the vegetable oil in a pan, wok or balti if you've got one. Season the chicken meat with a pinch of turmeric, cumin, chilli powder, paprika and salt then fry for 3–4 minutes. Remove and keep warm. Add the remaining oil then when hot add the onion, garlic, ginger and pepper and cook until lightly brown. Now add the remaining turmeric, cumin, chilli powder and paprika and the fenugreek (if using). Also add the chopped tomatoes, tomato purée and water and cook over medium to high heat for 10–15 minutes. Return the chicken to the pan and stir in the fresh coriander. Serve in the balti pot with tomato quarters on top and a sprig of fresh coriander.

TURKEY POCKETS WITH SPINACH AND CHEESE

SERVES 4

4 thick turkey steaks (about 1cm (½ in) thick)

4 slices of Gruyère cheese

100 g (4 oz) cooked spinach, drained well and seasoned with salt, and freshly ground black pepper and nutmeg

25 g (1 oz) plain flour, seasoned

1 egg beaten with 1 tablespoon of water

50 g (2 oz) white breadcrumbs

50 g (2 oz) butter

2 tablespoon olive oil

1 tablespoon chopped fresh parsley

Yummy is certainly one way of describing this dish. It's so easy to prepare and tastes great. You can use frozen spinach if you want but make sure it's well drained.

METHOD

Lay the turkey steaks flat on your working surface then cut a pocket into each steak, using a sharp knife, making sure you don't cut through completely. Slip in a slice of Gruyère cheese then 25 g (1 oz) of the spinach inside the pocket making sure you allow at least 1 cm (½ in) clearance on the inside edge. Dip into the seasoned flour then into the egg wash, shake off any excess and finally dip into the breadcrumbs shaking off any surplus crumbs.

Heat the butter and oil over a medium heat and fry the turkey until golden brown (or bake uncovered in a hot oven, gas mark 7, 425°F, 220°C with a knob of butter on top for 15–20 minutes). Serve sprinkled with chopped parsley and *Speckled Herb Potato Wedges* (see page 90).

HAM & TURKEY IN THE HOLE WITH A CRISPY CRUNCHY TOPPING

SERVES 2

225 g (8 oz) plain flour

3 eggs, beaten

400 ml (14 fl oz) milk

120 ml (4 fl oz) water

salt and freshly ground black pepper

85 ml (3 fl oz) vegetable oil

275 g (10 oz) cooked turkey, diced

275 g (10 oz) cooked ham, diced

75 g (3 oz) potato crisps, crushed

spring onions, trimmed and sliced on an angle

175 g (6 oz) fromage frais or natural yoghurt

This dish very much comes into its own around Christmas time. We all seem to have pieces of ham or turkey leftovers so here's an ideal way of using them up. If you've got any turkey fat use it on the base of your pan instead of oil. Serve with a nice rich gravy.

METHOD

Pre-heat the oven to gas mark 7, 425°F, 220°C. Beat the flour in with the eggs then gradually beat in the milk and water until smooth. Leave the mixture to rest for 30 minutes in the fridge. Remove then season, add 2 tablespoons of the vegetable oil and whisk again.

Mix the turkey, ham, crisps, onions and fromage frais together and season with about 10 twists of black pepper. Heat the remaining oil in a large roasting tin until very hot (you can do this in the oven), then slowly pour in the ham and turkey mix (be careful of any splashes – wear rubber gloves if you have to). Give it a quick spread then pour over the batter mix and return to the oven. Do this quickly so as not to lose heat. Cook for 20–30 minutes until crunchy and golden.

GOLDEN TURKEY **HOLSTEIN**

1 tablespoon chopped fresh parsley

25 g (1 oz) white breadcrumbs

salt and freshly ground black pepper

2–3 tablespoons plain flour

200 g (7 oz) turkey breast steak

1 egg, beaten with 1 tablespoon water

50 g (2 oz) butter

1 large egg

1 tablespoon capers

1 teaspoon lemon juice

4 anchovy fillets

urkey is fast becoming one of the main rivals to chicken. It has half the fat, is very versatile and reasonably priced. Holstein was a classic dish using veal but I think that turkey is a brilliant substitute. Use olive oil instead of butter for frying the turkey if you want.

METHOD

Mix half the parsley with the breadcrumbs. Lightly season the flour and dip the turkey in it (use a plastic bag), then dip in egg wash making sure it's well coated. Shake off any excess then dip into the breadcrumb and parsley mixture, pressing down with your fingers so the crumbs really cling.

Either melt half the butter in a frying pan and fry the turkey for 5–6 minutes each side or bake in a hot oven at gas mark 7, 425°F, 220°C for 12–15 minutes. Melt half the remaining butter in another small frying pan over a low to medium heat and fry the egg slowly, sunny side up. Put the cooked turkey on a plate and place the fried egg on top. Add the remaining butter to the frying pan, increase the heat and when it starts to brown add the capers, lemon juice and remaining parsley. Lay the anchovies across the egg and drizzle the flavoured butter over the whole lot.

CHICKEN LIVERS AND SLIVERS OF GARLIC AND WATER CHESTNUT ON CRISPY SEAWEED

SERVES 2

4 tablespoons good quality virgin olive oil

200 g (7 oz) chicken livers, drained

salt and freshly ground black pepper

½ teaspoon chopped fresh thyme

3 cloves garlic, peeled and cut into slivers

6 water chestnuts (use tinned), cut into slivers

4 teaspoons light soy sauce

chicory leaves

1 packet crispy seaweed or 100 g (4 oz) savoy cabbage, finely sliced and deep fried, dusted with salt and cayenne pepper

Chicken livers are a favourite of mine. They cook so easily, cost so little and are full of nutritious goodness. If you cannot obtain seaweed from the supermarket, ask at the customer service desk about them getting some in. They want your business, never forget that.

METHOD

Heat the oil in a frying pan until hot. Season the chicken livers with salt and pepper, thyme and gently fry until the livers are crisp on the outside but pink in the middle (normally this takes 1½–2 minutes).

Add the garlic slivers and gently fry for 30 seconds, then add the water chestnuts, and give the mixture a quick toss over a high heat. Now add the soy sauce and correct the seasoning.

Arrange three leaves of chicory on each plate, put a nest of seaweed or savoy cabbage on top followed by the chicken livers. Great with warm pitta bread.

MEAT

BEAUTIFUL BEEF COBBLER **LUSCIOUS LAMB STEAKS WITH SAGE BUTTER SAUCE** GLADYS'S IRISH STEW **CASABLANCA COUSCOUS** FA SCOUSE PIE **QUICK-FRY SOMERSET FILLET OF BEEF** MARINATED LAMB KEBABS WITH FRESH MINT CHUTNEY

BEAUTIFUL BEEF COBBLER

SERVES 4-6

275 g (10 oz) lambs' kidneys, diced

1 kg (2¼ lb) stewing beef, trimmed

4 tablespoons vegetable oil

1 large onion, diced

2 leeks, sliced

2 carrots, diced

1 parsnip, diced

2 bay leaves

4 tablespoons plain white flour

750 ml (1¼ pints) beef stock

1 tablespoon Worcestershire sauce

1 tablespoon tomato purée

SCONE TOPPING:

100 g (4 oz) butter

350 g (12 oz) self-raising flour

75 g (3 oz) Cheddar cheese, grated

**1 teaspoon fresh thyme, chopped
or ½ teaspoon dried thyme**

1 egg, beaten

about 200 ml (⅓ pint) milk, to bind

**salt and freshly ground black
pepper**

I was served this delicious cobbler whilst visiting a friend of my mother in Bridgend in Wales. Apparently it has been a family favourite for years and when you taste it you'll see why.

METHOD

Put the kidneys in a pan, cover with water and bring to the boil. Remove the scum, drain and refresh under cold running water. Season the beef, heat the oil in a large pan until hot but not smoking, then fry the beef until brown. Add the kidneys and onion and continue to fry for 2–3 minutes. Now add the leeks, carrots, parsnip, bay leaves and flour and give it all a good mix for a further 2–3 minutes. Stir in the stock, Worcestershire sauce and tomato purée. Season, bring to the boil and simmer on a low heat for 1½–2 hours. Heat oven to gas mark 7, 425°F, 220°C.

While meat is cooking, make the scone topping. Rub the butter into the flour until it resembles breadcrumbs, then mix in the cheese, thyme and seasoning. Combine with enough combined egg and milk to make a soft manageable dough, reserving a small amount of the liquid. Roll out the dough on a floured surface until about 1 cm (½ in) thick, then cut out rounds using a scone cutter or similar.

Once stew is cooked, pour it into a shallow ovenproof dish. Lay the uncooked scone rounds on top, slightly overlapping them. Brush with the remaining egg and milk mixture and bake for 12–15 minutes until golden brown. Serve with *Spicy, Sunny Savoy Cabbage with Bacon and Ginger* (page 96).

LUSCIOUS LAMB STEAKS WITH SAGE BUTTER SAUCE

SERVES 2

Salt and freshly ground black pepper

2 × 225 g (8 oz) lean lamb steaks

2 tablespoons olive oil

75 g (3 oz) butter

1–2 shallots or 1 small red onion, peeled and finely chopped

8 fresh sage leaves, cut into fine strips

4 tablespoons white wine or 2 tablespoons fresh lemon juice

sprigs of fresh sage, to garnish

Out of all the red meats, lamb is the sweetest, and fresh sage really brings the flavour out. This is a quick dish that also saves on the washing up.

METHOD

Season the lamb. Heat the oil in a frying pan, add the lamb and cook for 2–3 minutes each side over a high heat until nicely brown. Remove, put on a plate and keep warm.

Pour off excess oil from the pan, add 15 g (½ oz) of the butter, the shallots or onion and the sage. Gently fry for 30 seconds then add the wine or lemon juice. Reduce by half and slowly whisk in the remaining butter over a low heat. Turn off the heat, taste and adjust the seasoning, then pour around the lamb.

Garnish with a sprig of fresh sage and serve with *Sweet Potato Rösti* (page 93).

OPPOSITE (clockwise from back): *Superb Mackerel with Chilli and Herbs* (page 41); *Pretty Passionate Paella* (page 43) and *Portuguese Sweet-peppered Pan-fried Cod* (page 45)

OVERLEAF (clockwise from back): *Turkey Pockets with Spinach and Cheese* (page 58); *Rice and Peas* (page 102) and *Cashew Calypso Chicken* (Page 54)

GLADYS'S **IRISH STEW**

750 g (1½ lb) stewing lamb

1 litre (1¾ pints) lamb, chicken or vegetable stock

450 g (1 lb) potatoes, peeled and cut into 2.5 cm (1 in) dice

100 g (4 oz) celery

100 g (4 oz) carrots

100 g (4 oz) leeks

100 g (4 oz) white cabbage

1 medium onion, peeled

1 bouquet garni

1 × 400 g (14 oz) tin cannellini beans

1 tablespoon parsley, chopped

salt and freshly ground black pepper

This is a complete meal cooked in one pot. It's wholesome, appetizing and economical. In this dish I've used cannellini beans for substance and carrots to add a touch of sweetness, while both add texture and colour.

When I did my show on BBC Radio, 5 I went to cook for 70-year-old Gladys in London's East End. She wanted a healthy and economical stew and when she tasted this she said 'That's great, it'll keep me going all week'.

I've used stewing lamb here, but you could use chopped middle neck of lamb, which is cheaper.

METHOD

Put the lamb into a large pan, cover with stock and bring to the boil. Skim off any foam and excess fat from the top and leave to simmer over a low heat. Meanwhile, cut all the vegetables (except the potatoes) into 1 cm (½ in) pieces and add, with the potatoes and the bouquet garni, to the lamb. Increase the heat and bring to the boil, then reduce the heat and simmer for 35–40 minutes until the lamb is tender.

Add the cannellini beans and simmer for a further 5 minutes. Remove the bouquet garni and check seasoning. Sprinkle with chopped parsley and serve with hot soda bread.

OPPOSITE (clockwise from back): *Baked Potato, Pepper and Onion Frittata Frittata* (page 86); *Red Hot Broccoli Fusilli Forest* (page 78) and *Nice and Spicy Sweet Potato and Apple Bake* (page 83)
OVERLEAF (from back): *Casablanca Couscous* (page 66); *Quick-fry Somerset Fillet of Beef* (page 68)

CASABLANCA COUSCOUS

SERVES 4-6

2 tablespoons olive oil

Salt and freshly ground black pepper

450 g (1 lb) lean lamb, diced

1 tablespoon curry powder

½ teaspoon ground cloves

1 teaspoon ground cinnamon

1 large onion peeled and sliced

2.5 cm (1 in) piece root fresh ginger, peeled and grated

1 clove garlic, peeled and halved

2 carrots, peeled and cut into 2.5 cm (1 in) sticks

2 potatoes, peeled and chopped

2 courgettes, trimmed and sliced

275 g (10 oz) pumpkin, peeled, seeded and sliced

400 g (14 oz) tin plum tomatoes, roughly chopped

400 g (14 oz) tin chick peas

50 g (2 oz) sultanas (optional)

600 ml (1 pint) stock

1 tablespoon chopped fresh parsley

1 tablespoon fresh coriander

750 ml (1¼ pints) water

450 g (1 lb) couscous

2 tablespoons olive oil

1 teaspoon harissa

'Out of all the kitchens in all the world you had to come into mine.' Couscous is to North Africa what rice is to China, potatoes are to Russia and beans are to Brazil. Harissa is a very hot pepper sauce, available from good supermarkets and delicatessens. Use it sparingly!

METHOD

Heat the oil in a deep pan big enough for a colander to sit on top. Season the meat with salt and pepper then toss in the curry powder, ground cloves and cinnamon. Brown the meat in the oil, then add the onion, ginger and garlic and fry for 2 minutes. Add all the vegetables, the tomatoes, drained chick peas and sultanas (if using) and mix well. Pour over the stock, bring to the boil, reduce the heat, cover and simmer for 25–30 minutes until the meat and vegetables are tender. Stir in the fresh parsley and chopped coriander, taste and adjust the seasoning.

Bring the water to the boil in a pan and add some salt. Remove from the heat, stir in the couscous and olive oil. Cover and allow to stand for about 5 minutes. Transfer to a colander then place on top of the lamb stew, cover and steam over a simmering heat for another 5–10 minutes. Fork up the couscous to break up any lumps.

Mix the harissa sauce with the juice from the stew – about 3–4 tablespoonfuls will do. Serve the couscous on a plate with a well in the centre. Ladle in the stew and drizzle a little of the harissa mixture over the top – or a lot if you like it hot!

FA SCOUSE **PIE**

SERVES 4

450 g (1 lb) lean lamb, cut into cubes

50 g (2 oz) plain flour, seasoned

3 tablespoons vegetable oil

1 large onion, peeled and chopped

3 carrots, peeled and sliced or cut into cubes

2 large potatoes, peeled and cut into cubes

1 bay leaf

600 ml (1 pint) lamb or chicken stock (needs a strong flavour)

½ teaspoon black treacle

50 g (2 oz) frozen peas

egg, beaten with 1 tablespoon of water

salt and freshly ground black pepper

FOR THE PASTRY:

225 g (8 oz) plain flour

pinch of salt

100 g (4 oz) butter or half fat and butter, cut into small pieces

2-3 tablespoons cold water

I made this pie because I received a letter from a Liverpudlian who lived in Paris but hungered after English home-made cooking. He became even more desperate as Everton reached the 1995 Cup Final. Scouse pie has been around for many years and every household has its own recipe, but the meat is traditionally lamb.

METHOD

First make the pastry. Sieve the flour and salt, add the fat and, using your fingertips, rub together. Use lots of height to get air into it. When it turns to fine breadcrumbs, start adding water slowly. Blend together using a flat bladed palette knife until the dough leaves the side of the bowl in a ball shape. Pop in a plastic bag and chill whilst you make the filling.

Pre-heat the oven to gas mark 6, 400°F, 200°C. Toss the lamb in the seasoned flour. Heat the oil in a large saucepan and, when hot, fry the lamb until brown. Add the onion and fry for 2-3 minutes. Add the carrots, potatoes, bay leaf and the leftover flour, and mix well for 2-3 minutes. Stir in the stock and black treacle and bring to the boil. Then reduce to a low heat, cover and simmer for 20 minutes. Check seasoning. Remove from the heat, stir in the peas, pour into a pie dish and cool.

Roll out the pastry on a floured surface (large enough to cover the pie dish). Butter the rim and line with pastry trimming. Dampen the edges and cover the pie with the pastry. Trim, seal the edges and decorate with an FA Cup or whatever takes your fancy. Make a small hole in the top for steam to escape, brush with the beaten egg and bake in the oven for 25-30 minutes until golden brown.

QUICK-FRY **SOMERSET** FILLET OF **BEEF**

450 g (1 lb) frying steak, cut into strips

1 clove garlic peeled and crushed

2.5 cm (1 in) piece root ginger, peeled and grated

2 tablespoons light soy sauce

1 tablespoon clear honey

3 tablespoons olive oil

2 onions, peeled and finely sliced

1 green pepper, seeded and sliced into strips

1 plum tomato, seeded and sliced into strips

2 tablespoons tomato purée

2 tablespoons water

salt and freshly ground black pepper

1 teaspoon toasted sesame seeds

Yet another challenge set for me was to come up with a high protein menu for the Somerset 1st Cricket Team. This particular dish was their favourite and when I told them that fresh root ginger was great for joints, especially arthritic ones, the plates were licked clean. So was the next team! I've used frying steak here, but if you're feeling posh ask your butcher for fillet tail.

METHOD

Mix the beef with the garlic, ginger, soy sauce and honey. Heat 2 tablespoons of the oil in a frying pan, over a high heat. Fry the beef until nicely browned. You may need to do this in 2 or 3 batches. Set the beef aside and keep warm.

Add the remaining oil to the frying pan, add the onions and fry until they are lightly browned on the edges. Then add the pepper and tomato strips, and stir or toss over a high heat for 1 minute. Mix the tomato purée with the water. Return the beef to the pan and pour over the tomato purée mixture. Stir or toss, season with salt and pepper, toss again and serve on a pretty plate sprinkled with sesame seeds on top.

MARINATED LAMB KEBABS WITH FRESH MINT CHUTNEY

SERVES 3-4

1 boned leg of lamb (about 1.5 kg (2–3 lb))

MARINADE:

2 cloves garlic, peeled and crushed

2.5 cm (1 in) piece root ginger, peeled and grated

1 teaspoon chopped fresh coriander

1 teaspoon turmeric

1 teaspoon ground cumin

1 teaspoon mild curry paste or crushed dried curry leaves

1 tablespoon soy sauce

1 tablespoon lemon juice

1 tablespoon light sesame oil

2 tablespoon olive oil

salt and freshly ground black pepper

CHUTNEY:

1 large bunch fresh mint

3 tablespoons lemon juice

6 oz pine nuts

3 tablespoons clear honey

1 red chilli pepper, seeded and finely chopped

1 tablespoon crushed black peppercorns

The sun is shining, the days are long. What better reason do you need to light up a barbecue? So here's a dish that'll keep them coming back again and again. And if it's winter, just grill the kebabs instead. If you're using wooden skewers, soaking them in water for ten minutes before use prevents burning.

METHOD

Trim the meat, removing all the sinew and excess fat and cut into 2.5 cm (1 in) cubes. Mix all the marinade ingredients together, pour over the cubes of lamb and marinate for 2–4 hours, or overnight if you are organized. If you put it in the fridge, make sure it's covered so the smells don't affect other foods. To make the chutney put the ingredients into a food processor and blitz in short starts.

Thread the meat onto skewers – 6–8 per stick – and barbecue them turning every 3–4 minutes until sizzling brown on all sides. Serve with warmed, split pitta bread and spoon over the mint chutney.

PASTA

SINHALESE PASTA **SMOKED SALMON CREAM SEA WITH AVOCADO &**

TAGLIATELLE RED STRIPE LINGUINE WITH CHESTNUT MUSHROOMS & BASIL

PASCHICPEPMUSTOM 'CATCH UP MADDIE' MEATBALLS AND FETTUCINE

AUDACIOUS ANCHOVY, AUBERGINE AND GARLIC PASTA MAMMA TAHSIA'S

PASTA MEAT TREAT **RED HOT BROCCOLI FUSILLI FOREST** SMOKED BACON

CREAMED TOMATOES AND PEAS AND PENNE PASTA

SINHALESE PASTA

SERVES 2-3

450 g (1 lb) linguine pasta

salt

½ teaspoon oil

6 tablespoons olive oil

½ small onion, peeled and finely chopped

1 clove garlic, peeled and crushed

1 tablespoon curry powder

1 tablespoon chopped fresh coriander

1 tablespoon chopped fresh mint

1 tablespoon chopped fresh parsley

225 g (8 oz) peeled prawns

rind and juice of 1 lemon

freshly ground black pepper

This dish can be prepared in 20 minutes and makes a perfect light lunch or supper. It has also proved to be one of the most popular dishes I have prepared on the *Good Morning* show. Serve it with some crusty French bread and chilled lager. You can use spaghetti if you can't get linguine.

METHOD

Cook the pasta in a large pan of salted water adding ½ teaspoon oil. When al dente remove from the heat and drain. Heat the olive oil in a large frying pan or wok, add the onion and garlic and fry without allowing them to colour. Add the curry powder and stir-fry for 20 seconds then throw in all the herbs, prawns and lemon rind. Toss to heat through, then add the lemon juice. Lightly season with salt and pepper, add the cooked pasta, toss again and serve.

SMOKED SALMON CREAM SEA **WITH** AVOCADO & TAGLIATELLE

SERVES 2-3

450 g (1 lb) fresh or dried tagliatelle

salt

½ teaspoon oil

300 ml (½ pint) double cream

3 tablespoons Noilly Prat or dry white wine

225 g (8 oz) smoked salmon pieces, cut into small strips

1 avocado, peeled and cut into small cubes

1 tablespoon snipped chives

freshly ground black pepper

freshly grated Parmesan

Pasta is always a winner for a quick meal because it's full of goodness, extremely satisfying and takes minutes to prepare. Ask your fishmonger for smoked salmon trimmings which are a fraction of the price.

METHOD

Cook the pasta in a large pan of salted water adding the oil. When al dente remove from the heat and drain. In a separate saucepan, bring the cream and Noilly Prat to the boil and reduce to a quarter. Add the smoked salmon and avocado and half the chives. Lightly season, as smoked salmon is already salty.

Place the pasta in a heated serving dish and pour the sauce into the centre. Sprinkle the remainder of the chives on top and serve the Parmesan separately. A good white Muscadet helps it slip down nicely.

RED STRIPE LINGUINE WITH CHESTNUT MUSHROOMS & BASIL Ⓥ

SERVES 1

175 g (6 oz) linguine pasta

salt

½ teaspoon oil

3 tablespoons olive oil

1 clove garlic, peeled and crushed

100 g (4 oz) chestnut or brown mushrooms, sliced

2–3 sun-dried tomatoes, cut into strips or 1 fresh tomato, de-seeded and cut into strips

4 basil leaves, torn into small pieces

freshly ground black pepper

freshly grated Parmesan

Pasta provides more protein than either potatoes or rice, is low in fat and a good source of fibre. The essentially very healthy Mediterranean diet has lots of flavour without any butter or cream. Olive oil contains unsaturated fat that reduces blood cholesterol levels and reduces the risk of heart disease. Remember folks: it's never too late to change your eating habits!

METHOD

Cook the pasta in a pan of salted water adding ½ teaspoon oil. When al dente remove from the heat and drain. Heat the olive oil in a frying pan, add the garlic and 10 seconds later the mushrooms, fry for 1–2 minutes until the mushrooms start to weep, add the sun-dried or fresh tomato and basil leaves and toss. Add the pasta, season with salt and pepper, toss again and serve with a sprinkling of Parmesan cheese, a nice green salad and bread.

PASCHICPEPMUSTOM

450 g (1 lb) fresh or dried fusilli

salt

½ teaspoon oil

freshly ground black pepper

2 boned chicken breasts, skinned and cut into strips

4 tablespoons olive oil

1 clove garlic, peeled and crushed

75g (3 oz) red, yellow or green peppers (or a mixture), de-seeded and finely sliced

50 g (2 oz) button mushrooms, finely sliced

1 teaspoon chopped fresh tarragon

1 × 550 ml (18 fl oz) jar passata (sieved tomatoes)

freshly grated Parmesan, to serve

I thought this might catch your eye, and I bet you think it's the name of a little known Middle Eastern recipe I've just discovered. In fact it's a selection of abbreviations of cooking ingredients – namely PASta, CHICken, PEPper, MUShrooms, and TOMatoes. Fusilli are those pasta spirals which are great for the sauce to cling to. The recipe goes down particularly well if you have a glass or two of sparkling Saumur with it. You see, cooking is fun!

METHOD

Cook the pasta in a large pan of salted water adding ½ teaspoon oil. When al dente remove from the heat and drain. Season the strips of chicken, then heat the olive oil in a large frying pan. Fry the chicken over a high heat for 2–3 minutes, turning occasionally. Remove with a slotted spoon and keep warm. Add the garlic and peppers to the pan and fry over a medium heat for 30–40 seconds. Add the mushrooms and tarragon, and then stir in the passata. Bring to the boil and simmer for a few minutes. Return the chicken strips to the pan, then add the pasta and toss together to coat with the sauce. Season to taste with salt and pepper, sprinkle on the Parmesan and serve.

'CATCH UP MADDIE' MEATBALLS AND FETTUCINE

SERVES 4-6

450 g (1 lb) fresh or dried fettucine

flour

50 ml (2 fl oz) vegetable oil

MEATBALLS:

salt and freshly ground black pepper

450 g (1 lb) minced beef or lamb

3 slices of white bread, crusts removed

1 onion, peeled and grated

1 small clove garlic, peeled and crushed

1 teaspoon ground cumin

1 teaspoon chopped fresh parsley

pinch of dried oregano

1 beaten egg

SAUCE:

2 tablespoon oil

1 onion, peeled and finely chopped

1 bay leaf

2 tablespoons sugar

2 tablespoons white wine vinegar

1 × 400 g (14 oz) tin chopped tomatoes

1 tablespoon tomato purée

My children and their friends love this dish, perhaps because the sauce reminds them of tomato ketchup and the meatballs are like mini burgers. My son Jimmy, who's older, is always telling his baby sister Maddie to catch up, hence the name.

METHOD

First make the meatballs. Season the meat, soak the bread in water for a few seconds and gently squeeze to remove the excess. Mix all the meatball ingredients together in a bowl. Using wet hands form walnut-sized meatballs then flour them inside a plastic bag. Remove and slightly flatten, this makes it easier for cooking.

Heat the vegetable oil in a frying pan and fry the meatballs for 5–6 minutes turning 2–3 times. Do them in batches so you don't overload your pan. When cooked, drain the meatballs on kitchen paper.

To make the sauce, heat the oil in a pan, add the onion and bay leaf and fry for 2 minutes. Add the sugar and vinegar and boil for 3–4 minutes until syrupy (beware of vinegar fumes). Add the tomatoes and purée. Stir then cover and simmer for 15–20 minutes.

Cook the pasta in a large pan of salted water adding ½ teaspoon oil. When al dente remove from the heat and drain. Remove the bay leaf from the sauce. Serve the meatballs on top of the pasta with the sauce spooned over the top. 'Yum, yum, yummie,' as Jimmy would say.

AUDACIOUS ANCHOVY, AUBERGINE **AND** GARLIC PASTA

SERVES 4

400 g (14 oz) dried rigatoni (ridged tubes)

½ teaspoon oil

4 tablespoons olive oil

1 onion, peeled and sliced

3 cloves garlic, peeled and crushed

½ teaspoon chilli flakes (optional but nice) or cayenne pepper

450 g (1 lb) aubergine, cut into 1 cm (½ in) cubes

3–4 plum tomatoes, de-seeded and cut into strips

6–8 anchovy fillets, drained and chopped

6–8 fresh basil leaves torn into small pieces

1 tablespoon tomato purée mixed with 2 tablespoons of water

freshly grated Parmesan

This is certainly one for all those daring anchovy lovers. Each mouthful ignites your taste buds with a bold tantalizing experience. Vegetarians who occasionally eat fish might well like this dish. Use the tinned, salted anchovies in oil.

METHOD

Cook the pasta in a large pan of salted water adding ½ teaspoon oil. When al dente remove from the heat and drain. Mix in 1 tablespoon of olive oil. Heat the remaining olive oil in a pan and fry the onion for 2–3 minutes. Add the garlic and fry for another minute. Add the chilli flakes and aubergine and fry until lightly golden. Add the tomatoes, anchovy, basil and tomato purée, stir and cook for 5–6 minutes over a low heat.

Place the pasta in a serving dish, pour the sauce on top and sprinkle generously with Parmesan. A nice fruity wine helps it slip down effortlessly.

MAMMA TAHSIA'S
PASTA MEAT **TREAT**

SERVES 4-6

salt and freshly ground black pepper

450 g (1 lb) minced beef or lamb

3 tablespoons olive oil

2 cloves garlic peeled and crushed

1 onion, peeled and chopped

1 tablespoon chopped mixed herbs (preferably fresh), e.g. parsley, basil, oregano

175 g (6 oz) button mushrooms, thickly sliced

1 x 400 g (14 oz) tin chopped tomatoes

2 tablespoons tomato purée

85 ml (3 fl oz) red wine (optional)

450 g (1 lb) dried conchigle pasta shells

600 ml (1 pint) good beef or vegetable stock

2 × 150 g (5 oz) packets Mozzarella, thinly sliced in rounds

Italians eat the equivalent of 35 kg (5½ stone) of pasta per person every year; we in Britain consume about 25 kg (4 stone). I first tasted this dish when I was a teenager whilst visiting my friend's house and it still excites me today.

METHOD

Pre-heat the oven to gas mark 6, 400°F, 200°C. Season the meat with salt and pepper. Heat the oil in a pan and fry the meat, garlic and onion for 3–4 minutes, stirring occasionally. Stir in the herbs and mushrooms and after 1 minute add the tomatoes, purée and wine, and stir in the dried pasta. Pour in the stock, bring to the boil then transfer into a large ovenproof dish. Bake in the oven for 20 minutes, remove and lay the slices of Mozzarella on top and return to the oven for another 15–20 minutes until the cheese is golden and the exposed pasta crunchy.

RED HOT BROCCOLI
FUSILLI FOREST Ⓥ

SERVES 2-3

450 g (1 lb) fresh or dried fusilli pasta

salt

½ teaspoon oil

250 g (9 oz) broccoli, cut into little florets

6 tablespoons olive oil

2–3 cloves garlic, peeled and crushed

½ tablespoon dried chilli flakes or 1 tablespoon chopped chives

6 sun-dried tomatoes, cut into strips

4 black olives, sliced (optional)

freshly ground black pepper

freshly grated Pecorino

Pecorino is like Parmesan, but with a sharper taste that goes exceptionally well with dishes that have quite strong flavour – like this *Red Hot Broccoli Fusilli Forest* perhaps . . . Don't let the Pecorino put you off (use Parmersan if you have to) but, if you feel in the mood, buy it and try it!

METHOD

Cook the pasta in a large pan of salted water adding ½ teaspoon oil. When al dente remove from the heat and drain. Blanch the broccoli florets in boiling water for 1 minute and drain. (I steam mine in the microwave oven for approx 40 seconds.) Heat the olive oil in a large frying pan or wok. Add the garlic and chilli and fry on a medium to high heat for 20 seconds. Then add the sun-dried tomatoes, olives and broccoli. Stir-fry for 30 seconds. Increase the heat, throw in the pasta, toss, season and serve with grated Pecorino. A few bottles of Pils lager add a little something to this light, spicy supper.

SMOKED BACON CREAMED TOMATOES AND PEAS AND PENNE PASTA

2 tablespoons olive oil

4 rashers lean smoked bacon, rinded and cut into strips

2 shallots, peeled and finely chopped

75 g (3 oz) frozen garden peas

1 teaspoon chopped fresh tarragon

85 ml (3 fl oz) dry white wine

275 g (10 oz) passata (sieved tomatoes)

150 ml (5 fl oz) double cream or crème fraîche

275 g (10 oz) fresh or dried penne pasta

salt and freshly ground black pepper

½ teaspoon oil

freshly grated Parmesan

Like using up the end of cereal on top of a crumble, this gives you the opportunity to get rid of those few ounces of peas which aren't quite enough to make decent portions.

METHOD

Heat the oil in a pan and fry the bacon until lightly brown, then add the shallots, and fry for a further minute. Add the peas, tarragon and white wine, and bring to boil for 2 minutes then stir in the passata when it starts to bubble. Reduce the heat, stir in the cream or crème fraîche, cover and simmer for 8–10 minutes. Meanwhile, cook the pasta in a large pan of salted water adding ½ teaspoon oil. When al dente remove from the heat and drain. Taste and adjust seasoning in the sauce, you won't need much salt because of the smoked bacon. Mix in the cooked pasta and serve with lots of Parmesan.

VEGETARIAN

MARVELLOUS MUSHROOM STROGANOFF **AUTUMN ROOT VEGETABLES WITH**

HERB CRUMBLE CRUST NICE AND SPICY SWEET POTATO AND APPLE BAKE

RAGOUT OF VEGETABLES IN A YORKSHIRE PUDDING NEST PLANTAIN, PUMPKIN

AND CHICK PEA CURRY **BAKED POTATO, PEPPER AND ONION FRITTATA**

FRITTATA ROLL UP, ROLL UP SPINACH AND STILTON ROULADE

MARVELLOUS MUSHROOM STROGANOFF Ⓥ

SERVES 4

2 tablespoons olive oil

25 g (1 oz) butter

450 g (1 lb) mixed mushrooms (e.g. chestnut, oyster, shiitake, flat field and button)

2–3 tablespoons brandy or dry sherry or apple juice

1 large red onion, peeled and finely chopped

1 tablespoon paprika

250 ml (8 fl oz) vegetable stock

25 g (1 oz) creamed coconut, grated or chopped

200 ml (7 fl oz) crème fraîche or double cream

salt and freshly ground black pepper

1 tablespoon chopped fresh parsley

ushrooms are really meaty, especially the large variety. 'Absolutely marvellous' was Will Hanrahan's comment when he tasted one on *Good Morning*. Needless to say I wasn't surprised: it's always a great success and the red meat variety is never missed. Choose the variety of mushrooms you like – but this is a good combination. If you're feeling extravagant, use a mixture of wild mushrooms as well as a few of the following. Some of the mushrooms need slicing, but keep them quite thick or, if small, leave whole.

METHOD

Heat half the oil and half the butter in a frying pan and fry the mushrooms over a high heat, stirring or tossing to get a nice even colour. Add the brandy or sherry (or apple juice) and if you're feeling flamboyant ignite and flambé (watch those eyebrows and lashes!). Put into a dish and keep warm.

Heat the remaining oil and butter, add the onion and fry for 2–3 minutes, then stir in the paprika and after 30 seconds add the vegetable stock and creamed coconut. Bring to the boil and reduce by a third. Stir in the crème fraîche or double cream and let the sauce reduce until rich and creamy. Return the mushrooms to the pan, taste and adjust the seasoning, stir in the parsley and serve over nutty brown rice.

AUTUMN ROOT VEGETABLES **WITH** HERB CRUMBLE CRUST Ⓥ

1.5 kg (3 lb) mixed root vegetables (e.g. carrots, parsnip, turnip, celeriac, swede, sweet potato, potato), thickly sliced and cut into cubes

1 bay leaf

1 vegetable stock cube

75 g (3 oz) butter

1 onion, peeled and finely chopped

75 g (3 oz) plain flour

450 ml (¾ pint) milk

½ teaspoon chopped fresh thyme

4 tablespoons double cream

salt and freshly ground black pepper

CRUMBLE:

75 g (3 oz) butter

1 small onion, peeled and finely chopped

2 tablespoons chopped fresh mixed herbs (e.g. parsley, thyme, rosemary)

100 g (4 oz) white breadcrumbs

75 g (3 oz) porridge oats

25 g (1 oz) sunflower seeds

pinch of cayenne pepper or mustard powder

1 tablespoon lemon juice

salt

In Autumn, vegetables are available in abundance and also tend to be cheaper. Sweet potato gives this dish its distinctive flavour. The crumble also allows you to use up any leftover bits in the bottom of your breakfast cereals, sweetness permitting ... You can use the crumble mix on all sorts of vegetables.

METHOD

Pre-heat the oven to gas mark 6, 400°F, 200°C. Cook the vegetables in boiling water along with the bay leaf for about 15–20 minutes until tender. Drain and reserve 450 ml (¾ pint) of the stock and dissolve the stock cube into it. Put the vegetables in an ovenproof dish and set aside.

Heat the butter in a pan, add the onion and cook without browning (smell the sweetness as it sweats) for 2–3 minutes over low heat. Stir in the flour and cook for a further 2 minutes then slowly stir in the milk and vegetable stock. Add the thyme and double cream, season with salt and pepper and simmer for 8–10 minutes over a low heat.

Make the crumble crust. Heat the butter in a pan, add the onion and herbs and fry for 2–3 minutes over a low heat. Remove and stir in all the remaining ingredients.

Pour the sauce over the vegetables, give the dish a few taps so all the sauce settles, then sprinkle the crumble mix on top. Bake in the oven for about 25–30 minutes until golden brown and bubbling.

NICE AND SPICY SWEET POTATO AND APPLE BAKE Ⓥ

SERVES 4–6

3 × 225 g (8 oz) sweet potatoes, washed

4 × 75 g (3 oz) firm eating apples

75 g (3 oz) light muscovado sugar

½ teaspoon salt

1½ teaspoons ground mixed spice

40 g (1½ oz) butter, plus extra for greasing

4 tablespoons water

This delicious recipe is a great vegetarian supper dish, as well as being an excellent accompaniment to spicy pork sausages or roast pork with crispy crackling. Try to use sweet potatoes and apples that are about the same size in diameter.

METHOD

Pre-heat the oven to gas mark 4, 350°F, 180°C and butter an ovenproof dish. Cook the sweet potatoes, whole, in a pan of boiling, salted water until tender. Drain well and leave to cool. Peel and cut into 5 mm (¼ in) slices. Peel and cut the apples into 5 mm (¼ in) slices and place alternate layers of sweet potato and apple in the buttered dish. Sprinkle each layer with a little sugar, salt and mixed spice. Dot with butter, sprinkle over the water and cover with a lid. Bake for 20 minutes, remove the cover and bake for a further 10 minutes.

RAGOUT OF VEGETABLES IN A YORKSHIRE PUDDING NEST

Ideally, you need the wide Yorkshire pudding trays for this dish with four large wells. Once filled with the ragout, they make a warming winter meal, especially accompanied with crunchy, roast potatoes.

METHOD

First make the ragout. Heat the oil and butter in a large pan. Add the onions and fry until golden, add the garlic and cook for a further 5 minutes. Add the herbs and mushrooms and fry for 1 minute then add the remaining vegetables. Cook for 2–3 minutes over a medium high heat, then add the white wine, tomatoes, purée and stock, bring to the boil and simmer for 30–35 minutes. Add the water to the cornflour and mix to a smooth paste, pour over vegetables and mix throughly, cook for a further 2 minutes and season with salt and pepper.

To make the Yorkshire pudding, pre-heat the oven to gas mark 6, 400°F, 200°C, pour the oil into the tray and heat in the oven. Put the flour into a bowl and add the eggs. Gradually add the milk and beat until you have a smooth batter, season with salt and pepper and rest the batter in the fridge for at least 15 minutes. Remove from the fridge, whisk the batter and pour carefully into the heated trays and return to the oven. Cook for about 15 minutes or until the puddings are well risen and golden brown. Reheat the vegetable ragout and ladle into the middle of the Yorkshire puddings until overflowing. Garnish with a sprig of parsley and serve with crunchy roast potatoes.

PLANTAIN, **PUMPKIN** AND **CHICK PEA** CURRY

SERVES 4

4 tablespoons sunflower or vegetable oil

1 teaspoon whole cumin seeds

1 dried red chilli pepper, seeded and crushed

1 onion, peeled and sliced

2 cloves garlic, peeled and chopped

2.5 cm (1 in) root ginger, peeled and grated

1 teaspoon ground coriander

½ teaspoon turmeric

5 cm (2 in) stick cinnamon or ¼ teaspoon ground cinnamon

450 g (1 lb) pumpkin, halved, seeded and diced into about 2.5 cm (1 in) pieces

275 g (10 oz) plantain, peeled and cut into cubes

1 x 400 g (14 oz) tin chopped tomatoes

225 g (8 oz) cooked chick peas, drained

2 tablespoons medium hot curry paste

300 ml (½ pint) vegetable stock

1 tablespoon chopped fresh coriander

salt and freshly ground black pepper

1 banana

1 tablespoon lemon juice

No, you're not going to plant anything except lots of harmonious ingredients into a pot and when the diners are satisfied you can get them to do some gardening. Plantain is the daddy of bananas. They are much larger in size and are never eaten raw. Plantain can be cooked in different ways, depending on its ripeness. Green ones are suitable for plantain chips and stews, yellow for quick frying or curries like this and yellow-black for desserts. Don't be put off by the blackness – the starch has turned to sugar, darkening the skin.

METHOD

Heat the oil in a pan. Fry the cumin seeds for 5 seconds then add the chilli followed by the onion and garlic. Fry for 1 minute then add the remaining spices. Stir and cook for another minute. Add the pumpkin and plantain, mix until all is well coated with the spices and the vegetables begin to turn slightly brown. Add the tomatoes, chick peas, curry paste and vegetable stock, and stir well. Bring to the boil, cover and simmer for 20–25 minutes or until the pumpkin is tender and the sauce is nice and rich. Stir in the fresh coriander, and taste and adjust seasoning. Peel and slice the banana and toss in the lemon juice. Serve the curry in a bowl with sliced banana on top and a sprinkling of chopped coriander. Accompany with *Coconut Rice* (see page 103).

BAKED POTATO, PEPPER AND
ONION FRITTATA FRITTATA

FRITTATA

SERVES 4

275 g (10 oz) potatoes, peeled and cut into 1 cm (½ in) cubes

4 tablespoons olive oil

1 large onion, peeled and finely sliced

½ green pepper, seeded and sliced

½ red pepper, seeded and sliced

1 green chilli pepper, seeded and sliced

5 large eggs, beaten

250 g (9 oz) Ricotta

50 g (2 oz) freshly grated Parmesan

salt and freshly ground black pepper

So this is what the Italians do with their eggs? It's superb hot or cold and you can add any meat, fish or vegetables to it, it will support anything. Try it, it's lovely . . . Chilli peppers are rich in vitamins A and C. If you use a frying pan, make sure it is ovenproof – i.e., no wooden or plastic handles – and make sure it fits in the oven first. Instead of a spring-form tin, a deep metal tart or pie plate will do. You can even cook this on the stove, but baking gives a better finish and taste.

METHOD

Pre-heat the oven to gas mark 4, 350°F, 180°C. Parboil the potatoes in boiling water for 5 minutes and drain. Heat the oil in a frying pan and when hot add the potatoes and gently fry until golden, then remove with a slotted spoon and drain on kitchen paper. In the same pan, add the onion and fry until lightly golden. Add the peppers and chilli for 1 minute, remove with a slotted spoon and drain on kitchen paper.

When well drained mix the potatoes, onion and peppers with the beaten egg then mix in the Ricotta and Parmesan and season with salt and pepper. Pour into a well buttered, spring-form tin or an ovenproof buttered frying pan and bake in the oven for 35–40 minutes until the centre is firm and the top golden brown. (You can always brown it a bit more under the grill.) Loosen the frittata around the edge, turn out onto a plate, cool slightly then cut into wedges and serve with salad.

ROLL UP, ROLL UP SPINACH AND STILTON ROULADE ⓥ

SERVES 4

275 g (10 oz) spinach, blanched and well drained

salt and freshly ground black pepper

pinch of nutmeg

3 eggs, separated

225 g (8 oz) full-fat soft cheese

25 g (1 oz) freshly grated Parmesan

FILLING:

2 tablespoons crème fraîche or natural yoghurt

3 spring onions, trimmed and finely sliced

1 red chilli pepper, seeded and finely chopped (optional)

50 g (2 oz) walnuts, roughly chopped

75 g (3 oz) Stilton cheese, crumbled

TO GARNISH:

sprigs of watercress

slices of orange, quartered

This looks so attractive yet it is easy to make once you've cracked the method. And once you've made this version you'll find it works with all kinds of fillings like cream cheese with smoked fish, horseradish and herbs or cream cheese with peppers, pine nuts, tomatoes and olives.

METHOD

Pre-heat the oven to gas mark 5, 375°F, 190°C. Butter a Swiss roll tin 30 cm × 23 cm (12 in × 9 in) and line with greaseproof paper or baking parchment, and if using greaseproof paper brush with melted butter. Season the spinach with salt and pepper, and add a pinch of nutmeg. Beat the egg yolks with the cream cheese and season, then stir in the spinach. Whisk the whites until stiff but still soft then gradually fold the whites into the spinach mixture. Spoon into the prepared tray and bake in the oven for about 12–15 minutes, it should be firm but spongy to the touch.

Lay a piece of greaseproof paper on a flat surface, sprinkle with the Parmesan and turn the roulade out on top of it. Cool slightly (I put a cold damp cloth on top) then peel off the paper and roll up with the new greaseproof paper inside.

Mix the filling ingredients together until fairly smooth. Unroll the roulade, carefully remove the paper and spread with the filling. Trim the edges with a sharp knife and roll up again with the filling. Garnish with watercress and orange slices.

VEGETABLES

AUBERGINE PARMIGIANA **CAULIFLOWER POLONAISE** SPECKLED HERB POTATO WEDGES **DUTCH CAPUSANUS POTATOES** JERSEY ROYALS WITH CREAMY LEMON BUTTER AND CHIVES **SWEET POTATO RÖSTI** CRUNCHY ROCK SALT ROAST POTATOES **CREAMY GARLIC POTATOES** SPICY, SUNNY SAVOY CABBAGE WITH BACON AND GINGER **WILLIAM'S RED RUSSET CABBAGE** BRUSSELS YULE SPROUTS **CARROT & PARSNIP PURÉE WITH FRESH CORIANDER** AUBERGINE AND COCONUT YUM YUM **FIERY GREEN BEANS, COURGETTES AND BROCCOLI WITH LEMON THYME** RICE & PEAS **COCONUT RICE**

AUBERGINE PARMIGIANA

olive oil for frying

2 large aubergines, cut into 2 cm (½ in) slices

300 ml (½ pint) milk

50 g (2 oz) plain white flour for flouring

400 g (14 oz) packet Mozzarella, cut into 5 mm (¼ in) slices

10–12 large basil leaves

50–75 g (2–3 oz) freshly grated Parmesan

SAUCE:

2 tablespoons olive oil

1 onion, peeled and finely chopped

1 plump clove garlic, peeled and crushed

400 g (14 oz) tin chopped tomatoes

1 tablespoon tomato purée

4 basil leaves, torn

150 ml (5 fl oz) dry white wine

salt and freshly ground black pepper

TO GARNISH:

sprigs of fresh basil

freshly grated Parmesan

There are many uses for aubergines – the list seems endless. Grilled with salad, baked with cheese, fried with tomatoes, or even made into a caviar spread. I don't always salt mine before cooking unless they're past their best. If you blanch them quickly in boiling water before frying, they will soak up less oil, which is useful as they can be wickedly thirsty. This sauce goes well with lots of other dishes too.

METHOD

Pre-heat the oven to gas mark 7, 425°F, 220°C.

First make the sauce. Heat the olive oil in a pan, add the onion and cook for 2 minutes. Add the garlic, cook for a further minute before adding the tomatoes, tomato purée, basil, white wine and salt and pepper. Stir and bring to the boil, then cover and reduce the heat and simmer for about 25–30 minutes.

Heat the olive oil in a frying pan and dip the aubergine slices in the milk. Shake off any excess milk, dip them in flour and then fry in the hot oil for about 1 minute each side until lightly golden brown. Drain them on kitchen paper.

Layer the aubergine slices, Mozzarella cheese, tomato sauce and basil in a dish, repeating the process and ending up with aubergines and sauce on top. Sprinkle with the grated Parmesan and bake for 5–6 minutes, or cook under a moderate grill. Garnish with sprigs of basil and a little more Parmesan.

CAULIFLOWER POLONAISE

SERVES 4
150 ml (¼ pint) water
2 small bay leaves
1 tablespoon lemon juice
1 medium-sized cauliflower
75 g (3 oz) butter
25 g (1 oz) breadcrumbs
1 large egg, hardboiled and grated
1 tablespoon chopped parsley
salt and freshly ground black pepper

Bring this vegetable alive with a touch of crispness and colour.

METHOD

Boil the water with the bay leaves and lemon juice, add the cauliflower and cook for 5–6 minutes until the florets are crisp and not soggy. Drain and remove bay leaves. Keep warm. Heat the butter in a pan, stir in the breadcrumbs and fry until golden. Remove from the heat and stir in the egg and parsley. Season. Put the cauliflower in a dish, sprinkle with the breadcrumb mixture and flash under a grill for 2–3 minutes. Serve.

SPECKLED HERB POTATO **WEDGES**

SERVES 4
1 kg (2 lb) potatoes
50 g (2 oz) butter
2 tablespoons olive oil
2–3 tablespoons fresh mixed herbs, chopped (e.g. parsley, sage, rosemary and thyme)
salt and freshly ground black pepper

They say that the goodness in potatoes is only skin deep so here I keep them on. I bet you the herbs spark off a song.

METHOD

Cut the potatoes into wedges and cook, skin-on, in boiling salted water for 5 minutes. Drain. Heat the butter and oil in the frying pan. Add two-thirds of the herbs and all the potatoes and fry until crispy and aromatic. Season with salt and pepper and sprinkle the remaining herbs on top. Serve hot.

DUTCH CAPUSANUS POTATOES

1 kg (2 lb) potatoes, peeled and cut into about 2.5cm (1 in) cubes

50 g (2 oz) butter

6 rashers smoked bacon, rinded and cut into strips

1 tablespoon chopped fresh rosemary

1 onion, peeled and sliced

2 leeks, trimmed and finely sliced

120 ml (4 fl oz) white wine

150 ml (5 fl oz) vegetable or chicken stock

freshly ground black pepper

I've taken an old Dutch dish, added potatoes and a few herbs and the result is really quite stunning.

METHOD

Parboil the potaotes in boiling water for 8–10 minutes, until half-cooked but firm. Drain. Heat the butter in a pan. Add the bacon and fry for 3–4 minutes. Add the potatoes and rosemary and fry for 5–10 minutes stirring often so as to colour the potatoes. Remove from the pan with a slotted spoon and keep warm. Add the onion and leeks and fry until lightly golden. Add the wine and stock, bring to the boil and cook for 5 minutes over a high heat. Mix the potatoes back in. Continue on a high heat so the potatoes absorb all the wine and stock. Season with lots of black pepper and serve.

JERSEY ROYALS WITH CREAMY LEMON BUTTER AND CHIVES

1 kg (2 lb) Jersey Royal new potatoes

juice of 1 lemon

2 tablespoons double cream

50–75g (2–3 oz) butter, softened

1 tablespoon snipped fresh chives

salt and freshly ground black pepper

These kidney-shaped potatoes are usually packed in sandy soil. Their flaky skins should be gently wiped rather than peeled. They are in season from May for about 8 weeks and they really are, as the saying goes, fit for the Royals. My mate, Joe Royal, lives down the Old Kent Road.

METHOD

Cook the potatoes in salted water and drain. Warm a pan over a medium heat, add the lemon juice and whisk in the cream, butter and chives. Remove from the heat, season and splash over the potatoes.

SWEET POTATO RÖSTI

SERVES 4

4 rashers streaky bacon

225–275g (8–10 oz) sweet potatoes, peeled

225–275g (8–10 oz) potatoes, peeled

2 spring onions, finely chopped

1 teaspoon chopped fresh rosemary

pinch of nutmeg

salt and freshly ground black pepper

50g (2 oz) butter

3 tablespoons olive oil

This recipe shows the versatility of the sweet potato. When cooking, treat them like you would ordinary potatoes. They'll give a touch of sweetness to any dish and are full of iron. When selecting sweet potatoes, look for ones that are firm with no blemishes.

You can make individual röstis using a small amount of the mixture pressed into a scone ring to get a nice even size.

METHOD

Grill the bacon until crisp, crunch up into a bowl and set aside. Parboil the sweet potatoes and potatoes in a saucepan of boiling salted water for about 10 minutes, drain and leave until cool enough to handle. Grate both types of potato, add the bacon, spring onions, rosemary and nutmeg, and season well. Mix thoroughly. Heat half the butter and oil in a frying pan, add the potato mixture and press down to form a flat cake. Fry over a medium to low heat for 8–10 minutes until the base is golden brown and firm (use a palette knife to gently lift the edge and check). Loosen the edge and underside with a knife then turn the rösti upside down onto a plate. Heat the remaining oil and butter in the pan, slide the cake back in and brown the other side (about 3–4 minutes). Slide back onto the plate and serve cut into wedges.

CRUNCHY ROCK SALT ROAST **POTATOES**

SERVES 4

1 kg (2 lb) potatoes, lightly peeled for goodness sake

1–2 tablespoons medium ground rock salt

vegetable oil, for roasting

freshly ground black pepper

Potatoes are the most widely grown vegetable. They have a high nutritional value and when cooked like this you can eat them till the cows come home. Says who? Says me!

METHOD

Pre-heat the oven gas mark 7, 425°F, 220°C. Parboil the potatoes in boiling water for 10–15 minutes until the outsides just start to flake, but the potatoes are still firm. Drain well and sprinkle with rock salt. Heat at least 5 mm (¼ in) oil in the roasting tin in the oven. Put the potatoes into the roasting tin carefully to avoid splashes and add a few twists of pepper. Roast, turning occasionally, for 15–20 minutes until golden brown.

CREAMY GARLIC POTATOES

SERVES 4

1 kg (2 lb) potatoes, peeled and cut into 3mm (⅛ in) slices

2 cloves garlic, peeled and crushed

600 ml (1 pint) double cream

pinch of nutmeg

salt and freshly ground black pepper

25–50g (1–2oz) butter

Although this takes time to cook, the actual preparation is very easy. Best served with roast meats.

METHOD

Pre-heat the oven to gas mark 6, 400°F, 200°C. Rinse the potatoes under running water to remove some of the starch and pat dry. Butter an ovenproof dish and arrange a single layer of potatoes on the bottom. Mix the garlic with the cream and nutmeg and season with salt and pepper. Spoon over the potatoes to cover and repeat until all the ingredients have been used up. Dot the top with small nuggets of butter, cover with foil and bake in the oven for about 1½ hours. Remove the foil for the final ½ hour of cooking to give the dish a crispy topping.

SPICY, SUNNY SAVOY **CABBAGE** WITH **BACON AND GINGER**

SERVES 2-4

3 tablespoons olive oil

50 g (2 oz) unsalted butter

2.5 cm (1 in) piece root ginger, peeled and cut into fine strips

1 small red chilli pepper, seeded and sliced into rounds

3 rashers smoked bacon, rinded and cut into fine strips

150 g (5 oz) carrots, peeled and cut into fine matchsticks

275 g (10 oz) savoy or white cabbage, finely sliced

3 tablespoons soy sauce

2 tablespoons clear honey

salt and freshly ground black pepper

This is a great vegetable dish for the winter months, the mixture of bacon and ginger gives the cabbage a real kick.

METHOD

Heat the oil and butter in a wok or large frying pan. Add the ginger and chilli and stir-fry for 30 seconds. Add the bacon and continue to stir over a high heat for 30 seconds. Then add the carrots and cook for 1 minute. Add the cabbage, mix well and cook for 2–3 minutes, pour over the soy sauce and honey and adjust the seasoning. Serve hot.

OPPOSITE (clockwise from back left): *Vesuvius Confittoro Soufflé* (page 116); *Icky Sticky Date and Toffee Pudding with Caramel Sauce* (page 106) and *Denzil's Pancake Forest Feast* (page 107)

WILLIAM'S RED RUSSET **CABBAGE**

SERVES 6

50 g (2 oz) butter

1 onion, peeled and finely sliced or chopped

4 whole cloves or ½ teaspoon ground cloves

1 kg (2 lb) red cabbage, quartered, cored and finely sliced

2 pears, peeled, cored and chopped

2 apples, peeled, cored and chopped

3 tablespoons brown sugar

3 tablespoons white wine or malt vinegar

5 tablespoons water

People have often said to me that they're not confident enough to cook red cabbage, but once you've tried this recipe you won't look back. I like to use Williams pears and russet apples, but it's not imperative. This dish can be cooked on top or in the oven.

METHOD

Heat the butter in a pan and fry the onion for 2–3 minutes without browning. Add the cloves and red cabbage. Stir-fry for another minute, then add the remaining ingredients. Mix together, cover with a lid and cook over a simmering heat for 40–45 minutes or in the oven at gas mark 3, 325°F, 160°C, stirring occasionally. If it becomes dry, add a little more water. Remove whole cloves, if used, before serving. This dish is wonderful with lamb and flageolet beans with garlic.

OPPOSITE (from back): *Double Chocolate Mousse and Sponge with Raspberry Ripple Sauce* (page 123); *Fruit Mango Medley with Lime Cream and Flaked Chocolate* (Page 126)

BRUSSELS YULE **SPROUTS**

2 tablespoons vegetable oil

2.5 cm (1 in) piece root ginger, peeled and coarsely chopped

1 kg (2 lb) Brussels sprouts, trimmed and quartered

225 g (8 oz) carrots, peeled and cut at an angle

1 red pepper, seeded and sliced

3 spring onions, trimmed and sliced at an angle

1 teaspoon grated lemon rind

1 tablespoon clear honey

salt and freshly ground black pepper

1 tablespoon sesame seeds

One of those dishes that gets the Brussels used up. Great taste, visually exciting, quick and easy to prepare. If you've got some cranberry sauce left over, throw that in as well – no more than 3 tablespoons, though.

METHOD

Heat the oil in a frying pan or wok. Add the ginger for a few seconds, followed by the vegetables. Stir-fry for 4–5 minutes on a high heat. Add the lemon rind and honey, mixing them into the vegetables. Add water slowly if the vegetables start to catch on the pan. Season with salt and pepper, sprinkle with toasted sesame seeds and serve.

CARROT & PARSNIP PURÉE WITH FRESH CORIANDER Ⓥ

SERVES 4-6

1 kg (2 lb) carrots, peeled and cut into chunky pieces

450 g (1 lb) parsnips, peeled and cut into chunky pieces

salt

1 bay leaf

50 ml (2 fl oz) water

25g (1 oz) butter

1 tablespoon chopped fresh coriander

freshly ground black pepper

pinch of nutmeg

sprig of fresh coriander, to garnish

This vegetable dish is easy to prepare and adds rich colour to any meal.

METHOD

Place the carrots and parsnips in a saucepan with a little salt, the bay leaf and water. Cover with a lid and cook on a high heat until soft and tender. Check the pan regularly and add small amounts of water if necessary. The reason for the small amount of water is that you are steaming the vegetables in order to retain all the goodness. There should be no water left at the end of cooking. If there is, strain in a colander. Remove the bay leaf and pass the vegetables through a sieve or purée in a food processor. Return to the saucepan, add the butter, chopped coriander, salt and pepper and nutmeg. Reheat gently and serve. Garnish with a sprig of coriander.

AUBERGINE AND COCONUT YUM **YUM** Ⓥ

SERVES 4-6

8 tablespoons olive oil

750 g (1½ lb) aubergines, cut into 1 cm (½ in) slices

1 large onion, peeled and sliced

2 cloves garlic, peeled and crushed

6 tomatoes, skinned, seeded and chopped or 1 × 400 g (14 oz) tin tomatoes

1 teaspoon tomato purée

½ vegetable stock cube or 1 teaspoon vegetable extract

100 g (4 oz) block creamed coconut mixed with hot water to make up to 300 ml (10 fl oz) coconut milk

salt and freshly ground black pepper

pinch of nutmeg

2 tablespoons grated fresh coconut or desiccated coconut

Coconuts seem to be everywhere although in the Caribbean they aren't the furry brown balls we get here. I've used block coconut, available from supermarkets. If using a whole coconut, make sure you give it a shake before buying to check it contains liquid so you know it's fresh. With fresh coconut you need the same quantity of hot water as grated coconut mixed together and strained through a muslin cloth.

METHOD

Pre-heat the oven to gas mark 5, 375°F, 190°C. Heat 6 tablespoons of the olive oil in a frying pan and fry the aubergine slices for 6–8 minutes, turning once or twice until golden brown. Drain on kitchen paper to remove excess oil. Add the remaining olive oil to a saucepan and fry the onion for 3–4 minutes. Add the garlic and fry for a further minute. Now stir in the tomatoes and tomato purée and cook for 2 minutes. Mix the stock cube or extract with the coconut milk and pour into the pan. Season with salt and pepper. Add a pinch of nutmeg, give it a quick stir and simmer for 5 minutes.

Layer the aubergine slices in an ovenproof dish. Pour over the coconut sauce, cover with kitchen foil and bake for 20–25 minutes. Remove the foil, sprinkle grated or desiccated coconut on top and bake for a further 8–10 minutes. Absolutely yum yum.

FIERY **GREEN BEANS,** COURGETTES **AND BROCCOLI** WITH **LEMON THYME** Ⓥ

50 g (2 oz) butter

1 red pimiento, seeded and sliced

1 teaspoon chopped fresh lemon thyme

4 tablespoons water

1 small head of broccoli, cut into small florets

225 g (8 oz) green beans, topped, tailed and cut in half

2 courgettes, cut into batons 4 cm (1½ in) long × ½ cm (¼ in) wide

salt and freshly ground black pepper

Colour is often so important when it comes to food and this vegetable dish could quite easily take centre stage, it's so attractive.

METHOD

Heat half the butter in a frying pan and add the pimiento and thyme and cook for 3–4 minutes. Remove and set aside. Put the remaining butter and water in the frying pan and when it starts to bubble, add the broccoli and beans. Cover and cook for 3–4 minutes over a medium heat. The water should almost completely evaporate. Add the courgettes and add the fried pimiento and thyme. Toss for another 2–3 minutes, season with salt and pepper and serve.

RICE & PEAS

SERVES 6

225 g (8 oz) red kidney beans or gungo peas, soaked in water overnight or 1 × 400 g (14 oz) tin red kidney beans

50 g (2 oz) butter

1 clove garlic, peeled and crushed

2 tablespoons spring onions, trimmed and chopped

1 teaspoon chopped fresh thyme or ½ teaspoon dried thyme

1 small red chilli pepper, de-seeded and chopped

450 g (1 lb) long-grain rice

1–1.2 litres (1¾–2 pints) water taken from the cooked beans or water

50 g (2 oz) creamed coconut, grated or chopped

salt

This is regarded as the Jamaican Coat of Arms. The peas used are either kidney beans or gungo peas – not the standard green variety. This was my mum's special recipe. Gungo peas, also known as pigeon peas, are often used in soups, stews and curries. You can buy them dried or canned.

METHOD

Refresh the beans under running cold water. If using dried beans cook them in a saucepan covered with plenty of water until tender (about 1–1½ hours). Make sure the water is at a vigorous boil for the first 10 minutes.

Heat the butter in a pan, add the garlic, spring onions, thyme and chilli pepper and fry for 3–4 minutes. Add the rice and stir in the drained beans and either the cooking stock from the beans or the water. Stir in the creamed coconut and salt, bring to the boil then simmer over a low heat for 25–30 minutes.

COCONUT RICE

SERVES 6

25 g (1 oz) butter

2 spring onions or 2 shallots, peeled and finely chopped

225 g (8 oz) basmati rice

600 ml (1 pint) hot water or light chicken stock

1 bay leaf

25 g (1 oz) creamed coconut, grated or chopped

salt and freshly ground black pepper

There are many types of rice including short-grain, long-grain, basmati and arborio. You can make a feast of dishes with them due to its international popularity. I've used basmati here for its fragrance and quality although long-grain can be used. It goes really well with many chicken dishes and curries. The coconut aroma will get you dreaming of a tropical paradise.

METHOD

Heat the butter in a pan, add the onions or shallots and gently fry for 1 minute. Stir in the rice until well coated with the butter, about 2 minutes. Add the water, bay leaf and creamed coconut, season with salt and pepper and bring to the boil. Cover the pan and simmer for 12–15 minutes, until the rice is cooked and the water absorbed.

HOT PUDDINGS

STEAMED CHOCOLATE AND SPICED FIG PUDDING ICKY STICKY DATE AND TOFFEE PUDDING WITH CARAMEL SAUCE DENZIL PANCAKE FOREST FEAST RHUBARB RHUBARB CHARLOTTE CARAMELIZED UPSIDE DOWN APPLE TART PEAR AND BANANA MONEYBAGS CRÊPES SUZETTE CHARMING CHERRY CLAFOUTIS STEAMED ORANGE AND LEMON SYRUP PUDDING GOLDEN COCONUT TREACLE TART APPLE AND PEAR CINNAMON CRUMBLE VESUVIUS CONFITTORO SOUFFLÉ HOMEMADE CUSTARD SAUCE

STEAMED CHOCOLATE AND SPICED FIG **PUDDING**

SERVES 4

120 g (4½ oz) unsalted butter, softened

120 g (4½ oz) soft dark brown sugar

2 eggs, beaten

75 g (3 oz) plain flour, sifted

2 tablespoons cocoa powder, sifted

¼ teaspoon ground cinnamon

¼ teaspoon ground ginger

¼ teaspoon ground coriander

75 g (3 oz) dried figs, roughly chopped

This is a chocolate lover's dream. If you don't like figs, you can use dried dates or apricots instead.

METHOD

Beat the butter and sugar together until fluffy, then add the eggs. Stir in the flour, cocoa powder, cinnamon, ginger, coriander and figs. Lightly butter 4 teacups and spoon in the mixture. Cover the top of each cup with a piece of pleated greaseproof paper overlapping the rim by at least 2 cm (1 in), then tie a piece of string around the top of the cup and knot tightly to secure the paper. Place carefully in a large saucepan with 7.5 cm (3 in) of boiling water, cover and steam for about an hour, topping up with water if necessary while steaming. Check if cooked by inserting a small knife or skewer which should be clean when removed.

Serve with *Chocolate Custard* (page 117) or warm maple syrup.

ICKY STICKY DATE AND **TOFFEE** PUDDING WITH **CARAMEL SAUCE**

SERVES 6
200 ml (7 fl oz) water
100 g (4 oz) dates, stoned and chopped
½ teaspoon vanilla essence
⅔ teaspoon bicarbonate of soda
40 g (1½ oz) butter, softened
100 g (4 oz) soft brown sugar
2 small eggs, beaten
100 g (4 oz) self-raising flour, sieved
sieved icing sugar, to decorate
SAUCE:
50 g (2 oz) butter
50 g (2 oz) soft brown sugar
100 g (40 oz) golden syrup
1 tablespoon condensed milk
4 tablespoons double cream

If ever there was an irresistible gooey pudding this is it. To be extra naughty, serve with clotted cream or rich ice-cream.

METHOD

Pre-heat the oven to gas mark 4, 350°F, 180°C. Grease a pudding dish or six dariole moulds and line with clingfilm overlapping the sides by 5–7.5 cm (2–3 in). Place the water, dates and vanilla essence in a pan and bring to the boil, continue to boil for 2–3 minutes. Take off the heat and stir in the bicarbonate of soda.

Cream the butter with the sugar, then gradually beat in the eggs. Fold in the flour and stir in the date mixture until you have a smooth batter. Pour into the pudding dish or dariole moulds, making sure you have a good 2.5 cm (1 in) gap from the top to allow for expansion. Gather the clingfilm towards the centre and scrunch on top. Stand in a tray of hot water and bake in the oven for about 40–45 minutes, until springy to the touch. Lift the pudding(s) out, using the clingfilm, then remove the clingfilm, turn out of the dish or moulds onto a plate. Put all sauce ingredients, except cream, in a saucepan over a medium–low heat. Stir until syrupy, then whisk in the cream and serve with puddings, with icing sugar.

DENZIL PANCAKE
FOREST **FEAST**

SERVES 4

100 g (4 oz) caster sugar

3 tablespoons lemon juice

4 tablespoons water

40 g (1½ oz) butter

3 Cox's apples, peeled, cored and chopped

175 g (6 oz) mixed forest fruits (fresh or frozen and thawed)

pinch of cinnamon

2 tablespoons brandy or your favourite liqueur (e.g. apricot brandy)

1 tablespoon clear honey

50 g (2 oz) hazelnuts, roughly chopped

8 pancakes (see page 00)

crème fraîche or clotted cream, to serve

had to include this recipe as it was my first on the *Good Morning* show. It's ironic that the last time I worked with presenter, Anne Diamond, on TV AM many years before, I also made a pancake dish. She enjoyed it just as much this time. Pancakes can be made in advance, cooled, wrapped in cling film and stored in the fridge or freezer until needed. Forest fruits are a mixture of currants and berries, e.g., blackcurrants, redcurrants, raspberries, tayberries, etc.

METHOD

Heat the sugar and 2 tablespoons of the lemon juice with the water in a pan until you have a rich golden brown caramel. Watch over it carefully though, so it doesn't actually burn. Meanwhile, heat the butter in a frying pan, add the apples and fry until lightly golden. Add the forest fruits, cinnamon and remaining lemon juice. Increase the heat and when it starts to bubble, flambé with the brandy or liqueur (watch out for your eyebrows!) and then drizzle over the honey. Mix the chopped nuts with the caramel glaze. Lay out the pancakes, fill with the fruits and roll up. Put on a flameproof dish and warm under a grill for 1 minute. Pour over the nutty caramel glaze and serve with a dollop of crème fraîche or clotted cream.

RHUBARB RHUBARB **CHARLOTTE**

SERVES 6

75 g (3 oz) unsalted butter

450 g (1 lb) rhubarb, trimmed and cut into short lengths

rind and juice of 1 orange

50 g (2 oz) sultanas (optional)

175 g (6 oz) wholemeal breadcrumbs

1 teaspoon mixed spice

75 g (3 oz) soft brown sugar

50 g (2 oz) grated coconut (desiccated or fresh)

2 tablespoons clear honey

Rhubarb originally comes from India, China and Mongolia where it was known for its medicinal purposes. It's a very popular vegetable, not a fruit, and over 70% of the UK's crop is grown in West Yorkshire. Young and tender stems are good for bottling and older rhubarb for jam and chutneys. It's available from December to June, and a few new varieties as late as July. I've called this recipe *Rhubarb Rhubarb Charlotte* as there are two yummy layers of rhubarb. You can also use other fruits such as cooking apple, apricots and blackberries to make a charlotte.

METHOD

Pre-heat the oven to gas mark 4, 350°F, 180°C. Heat half the butter in a pan and fry the rhubarb for 2–3 minutes. Add the orange rind and sultanas and continue to fry until soft but firm. Set aside. Fry the breadcrumbs in the remaining butter until brown then add the mixed spice, half the sugar, and the grated coconut. Layer the rhubarb and breadcrumbs in a shallow ovenproof dish, finishing with a layer of breadcrumbs. Mix the remaining sugar with the orange juice and honey and pour over the top. Bake in the oven for about 20–25 minutes until rich golden brown. Serve with *Homemade Custard Sauce* (page 117) or cream.

CARAMELIZED UPSIDE DOWN APPLE TART

SERVES 4-6

50 g (2 oz butter), softened

100 g (4 oz) caster sugar

4-6 dessert apples, preferably Cox's, peeled, cored and halved

225 g (8 oz) ready made puff pastry

You can do many things with apples for a quick hot dessert. With a squeeze of lemon or lime, sugar and a pinch of spice, they can be transformed under the grill, in a pan or baked in the oven. Cook it in an ovenproof frying pan or a cast-iron enamelled dish. Alternatively, once you've caramelized the fruit you could place it into a deep round tart dish and roll the pastry over the top of the flat side of apples.

METHOD

Pre-heat the oven to gas mark 7, 425°F, 220°C. Rub the butter over the base of the pan, sprinkle on the sugar and sit the apples on top (rounded side down). Place over a high heat on the hob, shaking the pan occasionally, until the sugar turns to a light caramel. Roll out the pastry on a floured surface until it is large enough to fit the pan and carefully lay on top of the apples. Trim off any excess pastry. Bake in the oven for 15–20 minutes until the pastry has risen and turned golden. Cool for a few minutes before loosening the edge of the pastry with a knife and carefully turning out onto a flat plate that's larger than the pan. Make sure you spoon out any remaining caramel. Serve with cream.

PEAR AND BANANA MONEYBAGS

SERVES 4

3 pears, peeled, cored and chopped

3 bananas, peeled and sliced

½ teaspoon ground cinnamon

4 large sheets filo pastry

50 g (2 oz) butter, melted

25 g (1 oz) ground almonds

icing sugar for dusting

This is a great dessert for using up bruised bananas. When using filo pastry, always have a damp cloth handy to lay on top to prevent the pastry from drying out. Filo is the Greek word for leaf. The pastry is quite moist, so gentle squeezing will seal the top of each moneybag.

METHOD

Pre-heat the oven to gas mark 5, 375°F, 190°C. Mix the pears and bananas with the cinnamon. Brush each sheet of filo pastry with the melted butter and fold in half on the buttered side. Sprinkle a little of the ground almonds in the centre of the pastry, put a spoonful of the chopped pear and apple on top and pull up the corners of the pastry to form a 'moneybag'. Brush the outside with melted butter and chill in the fridge for 10 minutes. Place on a greased baking sheet and bake in the oven for 12–15 minutes until golden brown. Serve on a base of *Caramel Sauce* (see page 106) and dust with sieved icing sugar. A scoop of vanilla ice-cream is an added treat.

CRÊPES SUZETTE

100 g (4 oz) plain white flour

a pinch of salt

1 egg, beaten

300 ml (½ pint) milk

1 tablespoon butter, melted

vegetable oil

50 g (2 oz) butter

75 g (3 oz) caster sugar

rind and juice of 3 oranges

rind and juice of 3 lemons

12 pancakes

4 tablespoons Grand Marnier or brandy

TO GARNISH:

4 large strawberries; cut in half across the stalk

segments of orange

sprig of mint

A desert that never fails to impress loved ones, friends or yourself. Once I've squeezed the lemon, I stick a fork into the skin and use it as a stirrer. Of course there are many other ways you can use this basic pancake recipe.

METHOD

First, make the pancakes. Sieve the flour and salt into a bowl and make a well in the centre. Add the egg and half the milk, and beat until smooth. Gradually beat in the remainder of the milk and the melted butter until the consistency of the mixture is like single cream. Leave to stand for 20 minutes.

Lightly oil a frying pan and place over a medium heat. Slightly raise the handle side of the pan and pour in a little batter from the raised side. Tilt the pan until the base is covered and cook until golden brown. Toss or turn over and cook on the other side. Slide the cooked pancake onto a warmed plate and continue making pancakes until all the batter is used up.

Melt the butter in a frying pan. Add the sugar, orange and lemon rind and juice and bring to the boil, stirring with half of the juiced lemon attached to a fork for about 2 minutes. Place 1 pancake at a time into the syrup and fold up into triangles. Put the pancake triangles onto a serving plate. Add the Grand Marnier to the pan with the orange syrup and flambé to burn off the alcohol. Stir and reduce until syrupy and golden, then pour over the top of the pancakes. Garnish with a cut strawberry laid flat on the edge of each plate overlapped with an orange segment and spiked with a sprig of mint.

CHARMING CHERRY **CLAFOUTIS**

SERVES 4
15 g (½ oz) butter
75 g (3 oz) plain flour
75 g (3 oz) caster sugar
½ teaspoon salt
4 eggs
250 ml (8 fl oz) single cream
250 ml (8 fl oz) full fat milk
450 g (1 lb) pitted cherries
25 g (1 oz) caster sugar for sprinkling

Clafoutis is like a sweet version of Yorkshire pudding and it originates in France. If cherries are out of season, use the bottled or frozen variety, pitted if possible. However, there is no need to stop at cherries: pears, apricots and prunes are all charming in clafoutis.

METHOD

Pre-heat the oven to gas mark 6, 400°F, 200°C. Butter a large, shallow ovenproof dish or baking tin. Mix together all the ingredients, excluding the cherries, in a food processor or blender. Put the fruit in the bottom of the dish and pour over the batter. Bake in the oven for about 40–45 minutes until well risen and golden. Sprinkle with caster sugar and serve.

STEAMED ORANGE AND LEMON SYRUP PUDDING

SERVES 6

100 g (4 oz) self-raising flour, sieved

100 g (4 oz) white breadcrumbs

50 g (2 oz) suet

50 g (2 oz) caster sugar

rind and juice of 1 orange

rind and juice of 2 lemons

7 tablespoons golden syrup

2 eggs, lightly beaten

4 tablespoons water

Steamed pudding can often seem such a chore, but once you've got your ingredients together it really is very easy and believe me there's nothing like a home-made steamed pud! Use heat-resistant plastic basin moulds if you've got some as this makes it easier to turn the pudding out. Serve with *Homemade Custard Sauce* (see page 117) or a tin of your favourite custard.

METHOD

Mix the flour, breadcrumbs, suet and sugar together. Mix the orange and lemon rind and juice. Pour two-thirds of it into the flour mixture along with 4 tablespoons of golden syrup and stir well. Fold in the beaten eggs throughly. Grease a pudding basin or 6 individual dariole moulds and fill with the mixture. Allow 2.5 cm (1 in) at the top of the basin or 1 cm (½ in) at the top of the moulds for expansion. Cover with foil or greaseproof paper with a pleat across the top. Tie at the top with string and steam gently in a large pan of water for 40–45 minutes until light and springy to the touch. If using individual moulds, they will be cooked in about 30–35 minutes. In a small pan heat the remaining golden syrup, rind and juice with the water for 8–10 minutes until lovely and syrupy. Place the cooked sponge or sponges onto a plate or plates and pour syrup over the top. Serve hot.

GOLDEN COCONUT **TREACLE TART**

350 g (12 oz) bought shortcrust pastry

25 g (1 oz) butter

6 tablespoons golden syrup

50 g (2 oz) grated coconut

150 g (5 oz) white or brown breadcrumbs

rind and juice of ½ lemon

1 teaspoon cinnamon

This is a tart that's part of British country cooking. Every time I see it, my sweet tooth does the Jumpin' Jack Flash. Although they call it Treacle Tart, it's generally made with golden syrup. I've added a little coconut and cinnamon spice and it's especially good with *Homemade Custard Sauce* (see page 117), lashings of double cream or scoops of vanilla ice-cream.

METHOD

Pre-heat the oven to gas mark 6, 400°F, 200°C. Roll out the pastry on a floured surface. Line an 18–20 cm (7–8 in) loose-bottomed flan tin with the pastry. Chill for 5–10 minutes, then line with greaseproof paper and fill with baking beans. Blind bake for 15 minutes until set but pale. Remove the beans and paper. Reduce the oven temperature to gas mark 4, or 360°F, 180°C. Heat the butter and golden syrup in a pan then stir in the coconut, breadcrumbs, lemon juice and rind, and cinnamon. Pour the mixture into the pastry base and bake in the oven for 35–40 minutes until golden.

APPLE AND PEAR
CINNAMON **CRUMBLE**

SERVES 4-6

175 g (6 oz) butter, softened

3 apples, peeled, cored and quartered

3 pears, peeled, cored and quartered

50 g (2 oz) caster sugar

1 teaspoon ground cinnamon

3-4 tablespoons Grand Marnier or brandy

2 tablespoons lemon juice

100 g (4 oz) plain white flour

75 g (3 oz) demerara sugar

50 g (2 oz) rolled oats

25 g (1 oz) ground almonds (optional)

Crumbles are big business in my house, especially in the winter. I love using cinnamon to flavour puddings, especially those with apples and pears, as it stimulates gastric digestive juices.

METHOD

Pre-heat the oven to gas mark 6, 400°F, 200°C. Heat 50 g (2 oz) of the butter in a pan, add the apples, pears and caster sugar, then toss them with the cinnamon, cover and stew for 5 minutes. Add the Grand Marnier or brandy and flambé if you wish, but mind the eyebrows! Add the lemon juice and pour into a shallow ovenproof dish. Mix the remaining butter with the flour until it becomes crumbly, add the demerara sugar, oats and almonds, mix again and then sprinkle on top of the fruit. Bake in the oven for 25–30 minutes until crisp and golden. This is great served with whipped double cream, speckled with ground cinnamon.

VESUVIUS CONFITTORO **SOUFFLÉ**

4 eggs, separated

3 tablespoons caster sugar

1 tablespoon icing sugar, sifted

1 tablespoon unsalted butter

4 tablespoons warm red jam (e.g. warmed for 10 seconds in the microwave)

icing sugar for dusting

whole strawberries to garnish

For me this sounds so much more exciting than Jam Soufflé but, regardless of the name, the actual dish is delicious. If you want to be really fancy, heat a thin bar or metal skewer over a flame until red hot and after sprinkling icing sugar on the soufflé, gently make a few criss-cross markings on top.

METHOD

Beat the egg yolks with the caster sugar until light and pale. In a separate bowl whisk the egg whites and when just beginning to turn stiff add the icing sugar. Continue to whisk until stiff. Fold the yolks and whites together. Heat a large frying pan, add the unsalted butter and swirl around. Pour in the mixture and cook over a low heat for 5–6 minutes without stirring – and I mean low or it might catch and burn. Heat the grill on a medium setting before putting the omelette underneath it. Cook the top until golden brown and puffy. Make a fold line down the centre, pour on the warm jam and spread a little. Fold in half, slip onto a plate, sprinkle with icing sugar and garnish with fresh fruit such as strawberries.

HOMEMADE CUSTARD SAUCE

600 ml (1 pint) full-cream milk

1 vanilla pod or ½ teaspoon vanilla essence

4 egg yolks

40 g (1½ oz) caster sugar

2 teaspoons cornflour

85 ml (3 fl oz) single cream (optional)

ccasionally it is nice to serve a fresh custard sauce that you've made yourself. I know that it takes lots of egg yolks, but that doesn't mean the whites have to go to waste (see, for example, *Fabulous Passionate Pavlova*, page 124). If you do end up with a few lumpy bits in the custard, pass through a fine sieve before serving.

METHOD

Heat the milk (reserving a little) with the vanilla in a pan until almost boiled. Mix the yolks with the sugar and cornflour and the reserved milk until you have a smooth paste. Gradually pour in the hot milk, stirring all the time. Transfer to a clean saucepan, return to a low heat and simmer while stirring with a wooden spoon until the sauce has thickened and there's no taste of raw flour. For extra richness, beat in the cream before serving.

Variation: **Chocolate Custard Sauce**

For that extra special chocolate treat
Chocolate custard is hard to beat!

Make as above, but add 25 g (1 oz) cocoa powder to the egg yolk, sugar and cornflour and add a little extra milk. Add single cream at the end of cooking.

COLD PUDDINGS

BANOFFEE PIE

100 g (4 oz) ginger biscuits

100 g (4 oz) digestive biscuits

225 g (8 oz) butter, melted

1 teaspoon mixed spice

1 × 400 g (14 oz) tin condensed milk

300 ml (10 fl oz) double cream

4–6 bananas

2 tablespoons cocoa powder

When it comes to indulgent desserts, *Banoffee Pie* is probably one of the most delicious concoctions of sweetness you'll ever experience. Mouth after mouth of calorific explosions. Bananas take it to a new height. This energy fruit is full of vitamin E, potassium and carbohydrate. So . . . roll out the Banoffee.

METHOD

Crush the biscuits in a plastic bag with a rolling pin as finely as possible. Mix half the butter with the biscuits and the mixed spice. Press into the base of a clingfilm-lined 18–20 cm (7–8 in) flan tin, using a spoon. Chill to set.

Put the remainder of the butter in a pan, add the condensed milk and bring to the boil, stirring ALL the time – do NOT go off to answer the phone or anything, just keep stirring or it will start to burn. Reduce the heat and simmer for 5–6 minutes, slowly stirring, as it is very hot, until you have a light golden colour. Remove from the heat, beat in 2 tablespoons of the cream and leave to cool.

Pour the caramel on top of the biscuit base. Peel and slice the bananas and arrange half on top of the caramel. Put another layer of banana on top, sprinkle with cocoa powder using a sieve, then chill. When ready to serve, whip the remaining cream, spoon on top, dust with more cocoa powder and serve.

TIPPLE TRIPLE **TRIFLE** 125

1 packet of trifle sponges

3–4 tablespoons seedless red jam

1 × 300 g (11 oz) tin pitted cherries

1 × 300 g (11 oz) tin of raspberries in apple juice

120 ml (4 fl oz) sweet sherry

4 ripe bananas, peeled and sliced

3 eggs, separated

75 g (3 oz) caster sugar

350 g (12 oz) mascarpone

3 drops of vanilla essence

50 g (2 oz) toasted flaked almonds

Trifle arrived in Britain around 1600 and has been a favourite ever since. I called this 125 because it's so quick to make, like a fast train. I'm using sherry but, if you don't have any, use a drop of that holiday booze you've got at the back of the cupboard. Mascarpone has a creamy but firm consistency, is slightly sweet and can bring anything to life. Try it on toasted muffins with jam and it is great with fresh soft fruits like strawberries, raspberries and mangoes.

METHOD

Cut the sponges in half, lengthways and sandwich together with jam. Lay in the base of a large, china or glass serving bowl. Pour the tinned cherries and raspberries, including the juice, over the top and drizzle over the sherry, then lay the sliced bananas on the top. Whisk the egg yolks and the sugar together until pale and thick, then add the mascarpone cheese. Whisk the egg whites in a clean and dry bowl until stiff, then slowly fold into the egg mixture, adding the vanilla essence. Spoon over the fruit mixture and decorate with a scattering of toasted flaked almonds. Chill before serving.

THE **LEMON TART** OF **TARTS**

SERVES 6-8

225 g (8 oz) plain white flour

50 g (2 oz) icing sugar

150 g (5 oz) butter, cut into pieces

1 large egg, beaten with 1 tablespoon water

icing sugar for dusting

FILLING:

350 g (12 oz) caster sugar

4 large eggs, lightly beaten

rind and juice of 4 lemons

250 ml (8 fl oz) double cream

Always wash lemons before grating, and only grate the yellow skin, avoiding the bitter pith. I've used a sweet pastry mix, but if you're short of time you can use bought shortcrust pastry.

METHOD

Pre-heat the oven to gas mark 4, 350°F, 180°C.

Sift the flour and icing sugar together then rub in the butter until it takes on a crumbly sandy texture. Gradually add enough of the beaten egg and water until the mixture is well combined – you may not need to add all the liquid. You should now have a firm soft dough. The pastry can be made in advance and stored in the fridge, in a plastic bag, until needed.

Butter a 20 × 4 cm (8 × 1½ in) flan ring and chill (this stops the pastry from sticking when shaping it in the flan ring). Roll out the pastry on a lightly floured surface until about 5 mm (¼ in) thick. Place the flan ring on a baking sheet and line with the pastry. Trim and shape the edges and bake blind by lining the base of the pastry with greaseproof paper and fill with baking beans for 20 minutes in the oven. Remove the beans and paper and bake for another 5 minutes to ensure it's cooked. Leave to cool – do not remove the ring.

To make the filling, beat the caster sugar with the beaten eggs until smooth, then add the lemon rind and juice and finally whisk in the double cream. Pour into the pastry case, transfer to the oven and bake for 45–50 minutes until golden brown. Ovens vary, so you may need a little longer. Cool for a few hours before serving. Sprinkle icing sugar over the top and serve.

TEMPTING TIRAMISU

SERVES 4
4 eggs, separated
4 tablespoons caster sugar
450 g (1 1b) mascarpone
275 ml (9 fl oz) strong coffee (espresso is ideal)
3–4 tablespoons Marsala or coffee liqueur
24 sponge fingers (packet variety)
2–3 tablespoons cocoa powder

iramisu is one of my favourite desserts. It's often referred to as Italian trifle, which is not far wrong. Wonderful layers of sponge cake laced with Marsala-flavoured coffee are topped with creamy egg and mascarpone. For me it will always be very tempting. The name tiramisu comes from the Italian for 'pick me up'.

METHOD

Whisk the egg yolks and sugar until pale and thick, then beat in the mascarpone. Using a clean bowl and clean beaters, whisk the egg whites until stiff and gradually fold into the egg mixture. Mix the coffee with the Marsala, then dip half the sponge fingers in it and lay them on the base of a shallow serving dish. Do this one at a time and quickly, otherwise they melt away. Cover with half the egg mixture, place another layer of dipped sponge fingers on top and spoon the remainder of the egg mixture on top. Dust with cocoa powder, using a sieve. Chill and serve.

DOUBLE **CHOCOLATE MOUSSE** & **SPONGE** WITH **RASPBERRY** RIPPLE SAUCE

SERVES 6

75 g (3 oz) butter, softened

75 g (3 oz) caster sugar

1 egg, lightly beaten

50 g (2 oz) self-raising flour

25 g (1 oz) cocoa powder

1½ teaspoons baking powder

MOUSSE:

175 g (6 oz) dark, bitter chocolate

300 ml (10 fl oz) double cream

1–2 teaspoons coffee liqueur or brandy

50 g (2 oz) praline nut brittle, crunched up into pea-sized pieces

RASPBERRY COULIS:

225 g (8 oz) fresh raspberries

50 g (2 oz) icing sugar, sieved

splash of lemon juice

OR

1 × 300 g (11 oz) tin raspberries in apple juice

25 g (1 oz) icing sugar, sieved

DECORATION:

2 tablespoons cocoa powder

2 punnets raspberries

a little cream for ripple effect

The coulis used here can be used for many desserts such as tarts, sorbets, mousses and toppings.

METHOD

Pre-heat the oven to gas mark 4, 350°F, 180°C.

Cream the butter and sugar until soft and light. Gradually beat in the egg. If it starts to curdle, add a little flour. Sift the flour, cocoa powder and baking powder and gently fold into the mixture with a metal spoon. Do NOT over-mix or the sponge will bake unevenly. Spoon into a greased and floured 20 cm (8 in) sandwich tin and bake for 20–25 minutes, until firm but soft to the touch. Turn out and cool on a wire rack. Break the chocolate into pieces and melt in a bowl placed over a pan of hot (not boiling) water. Remove from the heat. Whip the cream in a large bowl until stiff and soft – not heavy – then whisk a third of the cream into the chocolate. Pour the chocolate into the rest of the cream, along with the alcohol and praline. Lightly fold in – do NOT over-mix! – keep it light, even if the mixture looks slightly marbled. Place the sponge inside a deep loose-bottomed or bottomless flan ring allowing at least 2.5 cm (1 in) for the mousse filling. Spread the mousse on top, using a palette knife to make the top smooth. Chill for 2 hours or more. To remove from the flan ring, wrap a hot damp cloth around the ring for 10 seconds then lift it away carefully. Sprinkle with sieved cocoa powder, then place one layer of fresh raspberries on top of the mousse.

To make the coulis, place the ingredients in a blender or food processor and blitz them. Then pass through a sieve and keep refrigerated. Serve portions of the mousse and sponge with coulis spooned around them drizzled with cream for a ripple effect.

FABULOUS PASSIONATE **PAVLOVA**

SERVES 6

4 egg whites

175 g (6 oz) caster sugar

50 g (2 oz) icing sugar

1 teaspoon cornflour

1 teaspoon white wine vinegar

FILLING:

300 ml (10 fl oz) double cream, whipped

about 750 g (1½ lb) mixed fresh fruit (e.g. strawberries, raspberries, blueberries, redcurrants, mango, kiwi fruit, pawpaw, pineapple, cherries, lychees)

3–4 tablespoons of your favourite liqueur (e.g. Cointreau)

TO DECORATE:

4–5 ripe figs, quartered

sprigs of fresh mint

3 passion fruit, halved (optional)

There's nothing like tasting the first fruits of summer. But as the days drift and fruit prices come down we can over-indulge. Pulp them up or pile them high on a delicious Pavlova base with figs for fun and passion.

METHOD

Pre-heat the oven to gas mark 1, 275°F, 140°C. Whisk the egg whites (use an electric whisk) until stiff, then gradually beat in the caster sugar until the mixture is glossy. Sift the icing sugar and cornflour together then fold them into the meringue, along with the vinegar, using a metal spoon (so you don't knock out the air). Pipe or spoon the meringue mixture onto a baking sheet lined with greaseproof paper or non-stick silicone paper in the shape of a circle with a raised outside edge to create a hollowed centre. Bake in the oven for about 1 ¼ hours until light and crispy. Cool, then carefully remove the paper and pipe cream around the edge of the meringue. Toss the mixed fresh fruit in the liqueur and fill the centre with them. Decorate with quartered fresh figs, sprigs of fresh mint and passion fruit, if using.

CHESTER'S CHOCOLATE & STRAWBERRY **ROULADE**

SERVES 4

4 eggs, separated

150 g (5 oz) icing sugar, sifted

50 g (2 oz) cocoa powder

1 tablespoon cornflour

50 g (2 oz) ground almonds (optional)

icing sugar for dusting

FILLING:

2–3 tablespoons sweet white wine or liqueur such as raspberry cassis

300 ml (10 fl oz) double cream, whipped

175–225 g (6–8 oz) strawberries

This is my father, Chester's, favourite dessert. Every time he comes to visit, he insists that it's on the menu!

METHOD

Pre-heat the oven to gas mark 6, 400°F, 200°C. Beat the egg yolks with 100 g (4 oz) of the icing sugar until pale and creamy (use an electric whisk). In a clean bowl and using clean beaters, whisk the egg whites. After 1 minute add the remaining icing sugar and whisk until stiff. Using a metal spoon slowly fold the egg whites into the yolk mixture. Sift in the cocoa powder, cornflour and fold in with the ground almonds. Do not over-mix – keep it light. Turn out onto a greased Swiss roll tin lined with greaseproof paper or non-stick silicone paper. Smooth over the top to about 1 cm (½ in) thickness and bake for 10–12 minutes until light and springy to the touch. Remove from the oven and cover with a clean, dry tea towel. Immediately turn out onto a wire rack, carefully remove the greaseproof paper and cool for 5–10 minutes.

Drizzle the wine or liqueur over the sponge then spread on the double cream to within 2.5 cm (1 in) of the edges. Cut two-thirds of the strawberries into quarters and scatter over the cream. Carefully roll up the roulade, using the tea towel to help guide it and place on a serving plate. Scatter the remaining whole strawberries around and chill until ready to serve. Dust with sieved icing sugar before serving.

FRUIT **MANGO MEDLEY** WITH **LIME CREAM** & FLAKED CHOCOLATE

SERVES 4

1 large mango, peeled and diced (saving the juice in a bowl)

1 punnet strawberries, hulled and halved

1 punnet blueberries

2–3 tablespoons rum, Grand Marnier or kirsch

juice of 1 lime

2 tablespoons clear honey

200 ml (7 fl oz) crème fraîche

1 chocolate flake, crumbled

The simple things in life are often the most pleasurable. This combination, without doubt, is a consuming passion. Well, so my wife tells me!

METHOD

Mix the mango, strawberries and blueberries together, pour over the rum and let the flavours infuse. Beat the lime juice and honey into the crème fraîche. Spoon the fruits into wine goblets, pour the crème fraîche mixture over the top and sprinkle over the crumbled chocolate flake.

Chill then serve or, if you can't wait, don't!